THE HUMAN PARADOX

by Leo Meyer

First published in Great Britain as a softback original in 2021

Copyright © Leo Meyer

The moral right of this author has been asserted.

All rights reserved.

No part of this publication may be reproduced, stored in a retrieval system, or transmitted, in any form or by any means, without the prior permission in writing of the publisher, nor be otherwise circulated in any form of binding or cover other than that in which it is published and without a similar condition including this condition being imposed on the subsequent purchaser.

Typeset in Archer

Editing, design, typesetting and publishing by UK Book Publishing

www.ukbookpublishing.com

ISBN: 978-1-914195-81-5

CONTENTS

Introduction 1

1. Time and Space 11
2. The Individual 61
3. Money 92
4. Morality 119
5. Religion 148
6. Education 177
7. Freedom or Stop making sense 196

References 226

ACKNOWLEDGEMENTS

First and foremost I would like to thank my wife Katherine, for putting up with years of philosophical musings and intellectual struggles which can't have been easy to live with. I would also like to thank the physicist and author Carlo Rovelli for allowing me to quote from his paper "Forget Time" and Benedetta da Lucia for all her invaluable help in editing the manuscript. Finally I would like to acknowledge the heroic efforts of thinkers such as Heroclitus, Nietzsche and Allan Watts who paid for their insight with their sanity.

INTRODUCTION

The world is a beautiful place, no one can deny it. Who has not been awed by an amazing sunset, the smile of a baby, a beautiful piece of music or simply the sound of lapping waves? Whether it is the natural world, or the man-made one, there are endless opportunities to be amazed by how special life is. It is also incredibly rare, and despite the immense size of the universe, according to our current knowledge at least, it only seems to have flourished on planet Earth. Yet in the midst of this incredible beauty, there is also, and has been for a long-time, unending suffering. Whether it is because of disease, pain both physical and psychological, loss, pollution, and natural or man-made disasters, humankind seems condemned to suffer in the very midst of paradise.

I, for one, have never stopped asking myself how this can be the case. In my search for answers I have gradually come to realise that this is a particularly human problem. Yes of course animals get wounded, suffer from natural disasters and kill and maim each other, but there appears to be little evidence that wild beings suffer psychologically as we do.

In this book I will try to explore what is different about humans and how that inevitably leads to this paradoxical situation. As a starting point for this process, I began by looking at many of our spiritual, religious and political traditions. However, what I gradually realised was that although there are a variety of explanations for why we behave as we do, what always seems to be missing is a rational reason for the origin of this paradoxical situation.

If we take the Judeo-Christian tradition, it is the story of Adam and Eve and their expulsion from the Garden of Eden, which provides the explanation. In this scenario the root of the fall is seen as man's curiosity to know and understand the world, rather than simply accept it as God's realm. This interpretation, ultimately relies on the existence of God, who created man and of course his polar opposite the Devil who persuaded man to take the step into self-awareness. Furthermore, the story of the Fall itself, doesn't explain how man ended up where he is but instead uses allegory to state what it is about human beings, i.e. self-awareness, that causes them to suffer. There is no attempt to explain what the self we aware of is actually made up of, and how that fits in with our perception of reality. If you are going to be a Christian, you simply have to accept that this is the way it is and that the best way to resolve the situation is through following Christian teaching.

The Buddhist Tradition takes a slightly different approach. The reason for our suffering which is explained in the second of the Four Noble Truths is put down to desire and ignorance. Desire is essentially the cravings we have for all those things such as material goods, pleasure and immortality, which will never actually satisfy us, whilst ignorance is the fact that we are not aware of our real situation. Although in a way this makes a lot of sense, what I never understood is how we got into this situation. As a result, just as in the case of Christianity, if you wish to try and deal with suffering you have to accept Buddhist teaching and follow the path it lays out. This is why most religious or spiritual traditions require faith. You have to be prepared to defer to a prophet, teacher or even manifestation of the Godhead, in order to be delivered from suffering in this life or the next.

Indeed, in many of these traditions and even other non-religious views of life, suffering is seen as a path to somewhere, or a lesson that will help us move towards a purer state of being. Christ's suffering is at the very core of Christianity and it was part of the process he went through in order to be reborn. This idea of life being a learning process, through which we can gradually improve our lot, is deeply rooted in our psyche. This is very much reflected in Marxist ideology where the suffering endured by the working classes at the hands of capitalism, is seen as ultimately leading to an ideal communist society.

However, I can't see that suffering brings any benefit at all, and there is even less to suggest that it happens for a reason. From where I'm standing "everything" does not happen for a reason, and we are not in some endless cycle of human improvement slowly leading us to "Nirvana". This is all psychological nonsense, designed to make us feel better about the fact that our lives can be so difficult. In fact, if anything, human suffering seems to lead to further human suffering and there are endless examples of this in human history, ranging from the wars of Ancient Greece, to the conflicts which still rage today.

The reality is that without cease people continue to cause suffering to themselves and others and in many countries, they even are prepared to risk death for a few dollars. There simply has to be a reason for behaving this way. From a utilitarian perspective it is totally counterproductive. Why would you in your right mind, spend your life struggling and striving to ruin both your own life and those around you? You might be thinking at this point "Hang on a minute, aren't you taking things a bit far". A lot of people spend their lives helping others, actually improving life. Of course, in one sense you're right, but how many people do you know, how many families have you come across, which do not have problems, hidden tensions and emotional suffering. Is it not quite a common occurrence, to come across a person, who is held up as a model of human behaviour, but who is later found out to have had some pretty serious weaknesses? Even Mother Teresa of Calcutta had accusations made about her. If she can have potential skeletons in the cupboard, who can't?

We seem to be just as blind when it comes to the effect we humans have on our environment. We spend all our time explaining why in technical terms we have got ourselves into such an awful state, and why it is likely that it will only get worse. We obviously blame consumption, but we never seem to ask ourselves why we have such a strong desire to consume, and why most likely we will continue. Even more importantly why, when it has been technologically possible for years to hugely increase our energy efficiency and massively reduce our levels of pollution without affecting our lifestyles very much, have we continued consuming and polluting on a gargantuan scale? The obvious answer is greed. But why are we greedy? What is it about us human beings that makes us want to accumulate, accumulate, accumulate even if it causes not only the environment, but also others and even ourselves to suffer?

The reason has to be common to all humankind. The particular reasons for an individual's suffering are not going to help us understand why it is a universal phenomenon. There has to be a fundamental flaw or perhaps contradiction at the very root of our existence, which leads us to suffer. For me there is no doubt that our "Egos" which according to the Oxford English Dictionary mean "a person's sense of self-esteem or self-importance" play a central role in this. It is all about us in relation to everything else, or simply us full stop. This isn't anything new you may say, psychologists have been talking about this for ever, and a fat lot of good it has done us. Well strangely enough, I happen to agree with you. Almost every psychological or self-help book published is about how to improve "your life". How to get happy, rich, feel contented, fulfilled or whatever. The common theme in all of this is you or me. Religions seem to be just as guilty of this. Some years back I spent some weeks in a Buddhist meditation centre in Sri Lanka. The centre, which was mostly full of depressed westerners searching for salvation, was led by a guru, who mixed western psychology with Buddhism. I had until that point naively believed that Buddhism was about meditation and dissolving the "Ego". However, I rapidly realised that "Buddhism", or at least the type of Buddhism being taught in this centre, was a path on which you embarked in order to at some point (possibly even in your next life) reach spiritual enlightenment. There were all kinds of different levels that you could attain through meditation, all another step on the ladder which had already been mapped out in the holy book. To me it seemed like another trick to persuade ourselves that we were improving, whilst continuing to pay homage to our ego. You could almost hear people's pride when they described to the teacher how they had got to such and such a place. I have nothing against this, and if it makes them feel better then I'm happy for them. But from my perspective, it seemed to be more about putting a plaster on the wound, and making the ego feel more secure than about understanding why we have an ego at all.

Almost everything that happens in life is about us in relation to others and almost every activity, belief system and/or spiritual path, or is about finding ways of making ourselves feel more secure about ourselves. Unfortunately, however much we try to improve ourselves, or live according to moral precepts, we cannot get away from the fact that we are acting in relation to our ego. As I have already pointed out, even those such as Mother Teresa who devote their lives to helping others probably still have some personal issues. These people usually suffer from the same self-doubt, and psychological suffering that permeates all of our lives. Is the root of the issue not the fact that we have a sense of being separate to others and the world around us? We talk about the environment, as though it is totally separate to us and seem to be unaware that not only do we affect it, but that we are actually part of it. In fact, a significant part of our own bodies are made up of foreign organisms. Indeed, according to a recent BBC report, human cells make up only 43 per cent of the body's total cell count. So in effect this idea that we are separate, independent beings, or in other words individuals, is actually nothing but an illusion and it is very hard to live an illusion 24/7.

What I am referring to, is the fact that we see ourselves as being separate and different from others and the world around us. As such we think of ourselves as individuals and project that individuality into the past and the future. In essence we have created an idea in our heads of what we are, and we then spend our lives acting in relation to that idea. The problem is not only that we have an idea of ourselves, but also an idea of the entire world, which fits into the same pattern.

The conflicts and suffering which I have already spoken about, are a direct product of the idea of separateness. If I didn't have an idea of myself being, for example, a Hutu, I could never have had the desire to eliminate my enemies, the Tutsis. It is only because I have identified myself as being part of a particular group, that I might then be prepared to assault a different group that I have been persuaded, is a threat to my own people and therefore my identity. As I have already mentioned, our identity is an idea, which exists in our head, and this in turn depends on having a concept of the past, the future, here and there. In essence we amalgamate all our experiences into our consciousness and then project this past experience to create a future notion of ourselves. This notion of ourselves only exists in our head, and is definitely not the same as the way others perceive us. How do we then reassure ourselves that our theoretical individuality actually exists in the face of the fact that it is fluid and often undermined by other people's behaviour?

INTRODUCTION

I am convinced that it is this drive to persuade ourselves of our own individuality and importance which is at the root of the human condition. In this book I am going to explore its different manifestations and look into whether it is inevitable. I will not provide you with any solutions but hope I may at least persuade you that it is an idea worth exploring. Life is the most extraordinary phenomenon and I feel that it is an unforgivable waste to spend it struggling to convince ourselves that the illusory "I" is actually real, rather than directly experiencing life as it unfolds moment by moment. This direct experience of life has absolutely nothing to do with the "ego", but rather means being a part of the world rather than an observer. From this perspective our existence takes on a completely different form. This state is actually at the core of our existence and it is simply not possible to live without it. So even though psychologically we may be strongly attached to our illusory identity, we also need to reconnect with our "real reality". Yet unless you are able to fully comprehend your actual situation, you are going to be limited to occasionally snatching a taste of this true freedom. Most of us have these fleeting moments, often completely out of the blue; where we feel that we are touched by something greater. For many this is viewed as a religious experience and it may be that many of those who feel that they have felt the grace of God are in fact simply experiencing life free of the veil of conditioning. It is an experience, which is beyond human understanding because it makes absolutely no sense at all. Our situation based as it is on our illusory notion of individuality is rooted in our need to make sense of the world. This is not a choice but rather utterly essential for our survival and is therefore hardwired into us via our DNA. As a consequence, even though we realise that there is something wrong with our situation, we seem to be almost completely incapable of realising that it is our perspective, which is the root problem. Instead, we spend our lives trying to improve ourselves. As we are trying to change something which doesn't actually exist, i.e. our notion of individuality, we end up rather unsurprisingly frustrated and often worse off than before. Even spiritual traditions such as Buddhism, which at first glance are based on the notion of dissolving the ego, end up falling into the trap.

But if we are able to understand the building blocks of our illusory reality, we have a much greater chance of truly understanding the origin of our predicament. Although this will not by itself free us from the chains of our ego, because we can understand where we are standing it will be a lot easier for us to shift our perspective and gaze on the true wonder of life in motion. I am going to start this book by exploring the most crucial elements of all in our "illusory" world: Time and Space. For it is these psychological concepts which have enabled us to create our entire worldview, and without which it would collapse instantly.

I. TIME AND SPACE

If we wish to understand why we behave as we do, we need to unearth the fundamental but hidden building blocks that underpin our world. One of the most basic is our belief in time, which in our daily lives we experience as a reality. We all accept without question the idea of yesterday, today and tomorrow. When we talk to someone about something that has happened in the past, we both know what we are talking about, and have no need to question its basis. Neither of us will find it necessary to say, "Please can you define what you mean by yesterday?" The same applies to all the different aspects of time. We all automatically understand its various measurements, i.e. years, months, days, hours and so on. Not only do we comprehend the concept, but it seems absolutely concrete to us. Obviously, we all know that yesterday no longer exists but there is no doubt in our minds that yesterday happened and can be defined within a time framework. This mode of function is automatic and almost no one could imagine living without it. In a sense we are not alone in this, as many other species, use observation and memorisation of repeating patterns in nature in order to live. Like us, animals live by nature's cycles and have patterns of behaviour adapted to night and day, the seasons and other natural rhythms. In addition, even though animals do not have a concept of yesterday and tomorrow, they are as affected as us by what has happened in the past. When my dog was young, he was badly hurt by a car and for a long time, he would keep well away from any moving vehicle. This is the basis of Pavlov's experiment in which a dog heard a bell being run, each time he was fed. Eventually the association became so strong that if the dog heard that same bell, he would start salivating even though no food was present. This type of learned behaviour enables animals to adapt to their surroundings and avoid potential problems. All of us rely on this in order to survive. A good example in the animal world is the mass migrations of the wildebeest in East Africa, orientated around the availability of grazing. These animals are expressing patterns of behaviour based on the memory of natural cycles. This type of behaviour is universal in the animal world and forms part of the most basic mechanisms of survival and adaptation for life on Earth. It also applies to behaviour that is not strictly linked to survival. We recently observed our dog learning to develop and repeat a game. He initially discovered that he was able to get his muzzle under a stick by digging the sand from under the middle part. He then started to throw the stick in the air and then twist around to try to catch it in his mouth. After repeating the process a number of times, he managed to catch it, thus perfecting his new game. Repetition, which is obviously based on using the memory of having done something before in order to do it again but more effectively, is at the very basis of animal and human behaviour. Bizarrely enough, the origins of the process that has powered human development into our high-tech era is no different to that of my dog learning to play with his stick. The principal difference being that scientists are not satisfied with knowing that a phenomenon will reproduce itself but wish to understand how it happens. Without our ability to memorise nature's patterns, we would never have been able to develop in the way we have. It seems clear to me that learning from the past in order to improve one's lot in the future, whether for reasons of survival or simply play, is at the core of human and animal behaviour.

There is clearly a major difference between how animals and humans perceive time. Animals live and are dependent on a time which expresses itself through natural cycles. They are not aware of it as a concept and they do not rely on that concept to live their lives. Yet for human beings, having a concept of time is absolutely essential. Simply put, because time allows us to imagine ourselves existing in different places and times, we are able to have a notion of ourselves separate from our environment, i.e. that we exist as separate beings. Without time this would be impossible as we would have no concept of yesterday or tomorrow. An individual who does not have a past or a future cannot have a concept of their own individuality.

Not only is time vital to the idea of our individual existence, but it is also the basis upon which all our social interactions depend. For example, if we do not all agree on what 10am on Tuesday morning means, the world would quickly descend into chaos. This belief in time is completely essential to the functioning of our world, yet we don't realise that we depend on it. Imagine if it suddenly disappeared from our lives; our entire world would collapse. No one would go to work, almost all travel would cease, children wouldn't go to school, and our economic and social systems would disintegrate. Without it our society would cease to function as it would be impossible to plan anything for the future, or to make sense of anything that had happened in the past. We would not be able to coordinate our activities with anyone else or even have a concept of them existing as separate beings! What I am talking about here is the idea of time rather than any kind of measuring mechanism. Obviously if we did not have a concept of seconds, minutes and hours we would be able to fall back on where we are in the day, i.e. sunrise, midday or sunset or whatever season we're in. Before the development of modern methods of measuring time, this is what people used. What is important is the idea that there is a past, a present and a future that have a linear connection and that can be used as a measuring stick to place us in the geography of our lives. As I have said, this concept is essential not only for us to function in coordination with others, but even for us to have a concept of ourselves as individuals. Without it we would simply live an eternal present with no past or future.

All of us accept this concept of time as a reality but from a purely logical perspective there is no reason to do so. I am not denying the fact that everything changes nor that there are observable repeating patterns of change in nature but rather that our perception of the world expressed through our concept of time is just that: a perception. We are not, like animals, simply using past experiences to improve our ability to survive. We are actively creating a world in which the existence of a psychological past and future are absolutely essential. For animals the idea that something will happen in a week simply doesn't exist.

Furthermore, because we live in a social world, time needs to be completely dependable and regular. So according to time as it is officially measured, our lives should run by at a completely even pace, much in the same way that if you go at a certain speed you will have covered X distance in Y amount of time. It would be of no use to us at all if it speeded up and slowed down at random. Yet the regular consistent unfolding of time that we all depend on for our societies to function is often in conflict with our actual perception of life. Perceived time is actually highly elastic – for example, it is commonly accepted that it flies by when we are enjoying ourselves and slows right down when we are not. People also remark on the fact that during our childhood, our lives seem to pass much slower than when we grow up, and we all have moments when time seems to last for ever and others when it seems to speed up.

However, this discrepancy between the time we experience, and its theoretical mode of function is not mere illusion but actually demonstrates its artificial nature. Strange as it may seem, even certain scientists are challenging the accepted notion of time. The great Einstein himself is quoted as saying in a letter to the family of his friend Besso after he died (1) "...for us physicists believe the separation between past, present, and future is only an illusion, although a convincing one". The Italian Physicist and Cosmologist Carlo Rovelli, who introduced the relational interpretation of quantum mechanics, states in his 2008 paper "Forget Time" (2): "Following a line of research that I have developed for several years, I argue that the best strategy for understanding quantum gravity is to build a picture of the physical world where the notion of time plays no role at all". He goes on to say in his conclusion "I could of course be wrong, but my own expectation is that the notion of time is extremely natural to us, but only... because they are features of the small garden in which we are accustomed to living (for instance: absolute simultaneity, absolute velocity, or the idea of a flat Earth and an absolute up and down)". This statement seems to be suggesting that our belief in the existence of time is as logical as the idea that the earth is flat. It may seem rather radical but needs to be taken in context. In order

I. TIME AND SPACE

to function in our world, we have to make sense of it. This involves working out the basic parameters of its function. If we take an absolute up and down – although from the point of view of physics, it may be totally absurd – as far as our daily lives are concerned it makes absolute sense. The fact that in Australia everything is reversed makes absolutely no difference, because from where the Australians are standing, up and down is also totally logical. The same can be said for absolute simultaneity, which suggests that events are able to happen at exactly the same time. An example would be: if I am talking to you, that we both believe that you are hearing what I am saying at exactly the same time as I am saying it. Yet because the sound of my voice has to travel, you are in fact hearing what I am saying after it has been said. The same is true for seeing. Because everything I see has to travel, albeit at the speed of light, before it reaches my eyes, what I am actually seeing are things that have already happened. However, our brains do not interpret it this way and as far as we are concerned, we are seeing things as they are. So, from the practical perspective of our daily lives, it is irrelevant whether absolute simultaneity exists or not. Yet although what Carlo Rovelli is saying may not appear to directly affect our lives, if we wish to understand how we function or how we interpret the world, his findings are extremely important. The way we perceive the world is at the very root of the human condition and as I have already pointed out, without time the individual cannot exist, and without individuality nor would our world. So, although it may seem that these scientific theories are just musings, what they are actually doing is digging down to the very foundations of our existence. It is then up to us to decide whether we take on board what they are saying or not.

Furthermore, Carlo Rovelli is not the first physicist specialising in this field to question our conventional view of reality. Quantum mechanics, which is the study of the very smallest units or particles that make up the universe, has been doing that since its inception almost 100 years ago. Whilst I am no scientist, my understanding is that these minute particles appear to behave in ways that most of us would consider impossible. Richard Feynman, the greatest physicist of his generation, said of quantum theory (3) "It is impossible, absolutely impossible to explain it in any classical way". One of the most famous quantum mechanics experiments is known as "the double slit experiment" where photons are fired from a projector through two slits onto a detector screen. The first extraordinary thing that this experiment appears to demonstrate, is that light particles or photons, are able to go through two slits simultaneously. Or in other words, something is able to be in two places at the same time! Logically this should be totally impossible.

Another experiment in quantum mechanics known as the EPR paradox is equally astounding. It shows that a pair of protons (one of the smallest building blocks in our universe), which are associated together in what is known as a "singlet state", will if separated even by a great distance act as though they are still attached.

I. TIME AND SPACE

They always have opposite spins and if the spin of one separated proton is measured, a reaction will be detectable in its pair instantaneously. This has been done with a distance of 10 miles, and theoretically it would still happen if they were separated by a distance measured in light years. Something here is taking place at faster than the speed of light, although exactly what seems to be a matter of some debate. Both time and space as we imagine them in the conventional sense seem to disappear completely. How is it possible for two particles to communicate with each other instantaneously even if they are light years apart? From our conventional view of the world, it is simply not possible. The problem is the same as the one posed by the double slit experiment. The universe at its very smallest level, does not behave in a way which can be explained by our conventional view of reality.

As I have already pointed out, the fault is not with the experiments but rather with the fact that our view of reality is not equipped to explain these results. The problem we face is that if we begin to question the validity of our reality, our world can quickly feel very unstable and irrational. Einstein was so disgusted by the whole notion that he made his famous remark (4), "Quantum mechanics is very impressive. But an inner voice tells me that it is not yet the real thing. The theory produces a good deal but hardly brings us closer to the secrets of the Old One. I am at all events convinced that He does not play dice". Whether any sense or not can be made of these experiments, it is clear that our conventional notion of reality has no place in the field of quantum mechanics. And lest we are tempted to say that it is all very well, but it doesn't apply to our lives, quantum theory is used in many applications, including television and computers, and even explains the nuclear processes taking place inside stars.

So it seems that science, until quite recently the very bedrock of our rational view of the world, has been discovering that our reality is not as real as we thought. In the world of quantum theory, things can be in two places at the same time, and communicate faster than the speed of light. It really is the world of Alice in Wonderland. As Carlo Rovelli has already clearly stated, the classical view of reality is merely what appears to make the most sense from where we are standing. In order for us to have become the most successful species on this earth, we didn't spend our time indulging in existential questions about the "real nature" of time and space. We have simply accepted our view of reality as "real" and got on with being successful.

I hope it is gradually becoming clear that time as we use it, is purely conceptual, i.e. it only exists as a shared concept between people. It is not the solid unquestionable foundation of our world that we all accept but a variable and relative measurement of the rate of change. All we have done is taken the rate of change of one substance and decided that it can be applied to everything. The reality is that everything changes at different rates and in many cases the

I. TIME AND SPACE

rate of change is quite variable depending on the circumstances. In fact, Einstein's general theory of relativity, which is now almost one hundred years old, demonstrated that the passage of time is affected by both speed and gravitational forces. So, for example, someone standing on Everest will age at a different rate to someone at sea level. What is difficult for us to accept is that we are not at the centre of the world and that the changes we perceive are not universal ones.

Inevitably this is all very paradoxical as there are so many apparently concrete examples of the existence of time, such as the internal clocks that govern most of the rhythms that we observe in nature. What it all comes down to is a question of perception; the fact that rhythms exist does not mean that we can extrapolate the existence of universal time from them. In short, there is no fixed time that we can all refer to, but endless different rates of change which themselves are dependent on a multitude of variable factors. Paradoxically the most crucial element here is not even whether time actually exists or not, but the fact that we are aware of it or more precisely believe in its existence, and that that belief is vital to us psychologically and socially.

Our perception of time has allowed us to take things a lot further than animals; because once we understand how something works and the mechanisms behind it, we use that process for our own ends. An excellent example of this is fire. Instead of simply being afraid of it, we learnt how to use it and even how to start one. This process bizarrely enough depends on the existence of time, because just as with our individuality we need to separate out fire as a concept that exists independently of its immediate environment. This way we can have the intention of building a fire in our heads with an idea of what it will be like in the future. The capacity to do this has hugely increased our ability to survive in different environments and speeded up the process of separating ourselves off from nature. One of the most significant developments in human history is farming, something which is simply unimaginable without the ability to learn from the past and plan ahead. It requires a knowledge of the seasons, how to prepare the soil, how to plant, weed, harvest and process the food. It has also required the development of various technologies, namely the plough and the grindstone. This would obviously have been impossible to develop without a concept of doing something which will be of benefit at some time in the future. Gradually this process has become more and more developed and has increasingly allowed us to dominate our environment. It has allowed far greater numbers of humans to live in one place than could ever have existed with hunter gathering. Without it there is no way that the modern world would exist.

What all learned behaviour, based as it is on a belief in a time-based world, has in common, is an implicit acceptance of cause and effect as the basis for action. If a process is observed to repeat itself then it is worthy of scientific investigation and our belief is that a valid process of cause and effect will be discovered to be behind it. When my dog digs under his stick, flicks the stick in the air and leaps up to catch it, he is unconsciously accepting it as the underlying connecting principle. The cause has to happen before the effect! If I have an accident such as falling off a horse and break a bone as a result, I first have to ride the horse, then fall off and break my bone. It would not be logical if breaking my bone happened before getting on the horse or at least I would not then be able to claim that I injured myself as a result of falling off a horse. Cause and effect, like its bedfellow time, are so deeply engrained in our society that it affects every aspect of it without us realising that it is the case. When you decide to do something, you use cause and effect in order to achieve it. If, for example, you decide to go shopping, you can imagine in your head a whole series of actions and events linked by time which will be necessary in order for you to return home with your bags full of shopping. Or if it turns out that your shopping trip did not pan out in the way you expected, you are then able in retrospect to explain the chain of events which actually unfolded. Even if we disagree on what the cause or causes are, there is never any disagreement about the underlying mechanism. We might even admit that we don't actually know what caused something, but this does not mean that we don't believe that a cause exists; we just haven't managed to discover what it is yet. This is wonderfully summed up in the medical word "idiopathic" which roughly means of no known cause. Although as I have already pointed out, animals use cause and effect as the basis for their actions, its sphere is much more limited. The human world is much larger and more complex because through the concepts of time and the three dimensions, we have created an enormous world stretching back into the past, far into the future and into places which we are not physically in contact with. This means that the sphere in which cause and effect can be applied is absolutely huge. Even if you take a relatively simple event such as a heart attack, the causes can be complex. You can talk about the physical causes such as the build-up of cholesterol, raised blood pressure and the resultant furring up of arteries. Yet even with all these causal factors present, it is often impossible to know why a heart attack happened at a particular moment. We have all heard of someone who is given the all-clear after having had his heart checked but goes on to die of a heart attack shortly afterwards. Equally one hears of people who have been told that they only have months to live but in fact stay alive and healthy for many more years. I have personally met quite a few women who have been told that they can never have children naturally, because, for example, their fallopian tubes are blocked, yet after one successful IVF baby go on to have one or more naturally. Of course, it is possible to say that just because we give a wrong diagnosis, this doesn't mean that cause and effect isn't valid. But even if this is true, it doesn't alter the fact that life is incredibly complex and involves innumerable interactions and connections which are often incomprehensible. When we move onto more complex events such as wars or disease epidemics, it becomes almost impossible to work out the causes or at the very least there will always

I. TIME AND SPACE

be a lot of disagreement. Furthermore, science itself has demonstrated that there are a number of situations, i.e. in the field of quantum mechanics, where its function appears to break down or be supplanted by something else. Yet despite this there are many of us who are completely unable to imagine any other way of viewing life and are extremely quick to react when they feel that their reality is threatened.

Indeed, anything that doesn't fit into the orthodox view of our world is quickly described as being all in the mind, whether it is telepathy, hands on healing or ghosts. And of course, what "all in the mind" really means is "out of your mind"! This behaviour is not new and has repeated itself historically. It just happens to be that "science" or at least the Darwinian version, is the new religious orthodoxy and it feels as easily threatened as the Catholic Church did during the inquisition. This is illustrated by the case of Galileo who was persecuted because of his support of the *Copernican system*.[1]

---

[1] The Copernican system stated that the world revolved around the sun. The orthodox belief was that the Earth was at the centre of the solar system and that everything revolved around it. The powers that be felt hugely threatened by this discovery because it put into question their whole world view and as such Galileo's position was viewed as having no basis in reality. At that time everything including God was very much based on a human-centric view of the world. The idea that everything did not revolve around the world, but that the world revolved around the sun, put into question the idea that man was at the centre of the universe. Today's scientific opposition to alternative medicine is similar to the Church's position versus Galileo, in as much as in both cases the status quo is threatened. Of course the crazy thing about that is that in recent years the Pope has rehabilitated him. What was once considered heresy has now become orthodoxy.

The same can be said about alternative medicine today, which is constantly attacked by the scientific community as being unscientific.

Perhaps this is not so surprising as "our time-based reality" really seems to work and fit together. We have developed a world full of computers, cars, electricity and myriad other technological, scientific and medical developments. In our daily lives we are swamped by evidence of the reality and rationality of our world. It therefore seems completely inconceivable that it could all be based on illusions, that it could be a giant con trick. If our world works well enough for us to build all these technological marvels, it must be real. It is totally undeniable that our perception of time has enabled us to master our world to the most extraordinary extent and allowed us to believe that we are individuals in control of our lives. However, the flip side of this is, that the greater our apparent control, the larger the shock when things go wrong. In less developed societies people seem to be able to cope with natural disasters much more easily, at least on a psychological level, than in developed ones. In my opinion this is not because they value life less but because they often don't believe that they are in control. This is probably because death and illness are much more part of their daily lives and because if there is not much that they can do about it, they have to get used to it. In developed countries we believe that we have a right to good health and a comfortable life. Furthermore, we rarely see death, disability or even much old age. The disabled and the

I. TIME AND SPACE

very old are usually institutionalised and invisible. We therefore live in a cut off bubble, where our created reality is totally dominant. This is how the notion of individuality has developed to a point where we are able to live as though our environment had almost nothing to do with us.

Technology such as the internet, TV, central heating and aeroplane travel exaggerates this situation as we seem to live out of nature's realm. When I trekked through the Moroccan mountains recently, many people still lived in almost medieval conditions and in many places, there was no running water, electricity, roads or any other sign of modern life. For these people nature and its rhythms totally dominated their lives. A poor harvest or a flood could destroy them. Yet for us in the developed world, we appear to be insulated from all of this and we are quickly reduced to a state of shock if something unexpected, such as an accident or natural disaster, happens.

Over the years, due to our ability to memorise and plan, we have increasingly been able to understand and master our environment, and in the modern era this has reached extraordinary levels. It appears we are now actually able to alter the genetic makeup of plants and even animals. However, the fact that we are able to do these things does not mean that we understand everything. Actually, we only see what we want to see, or more precisely the aspects of our world which fit in with our reality. These aspects exist, but as part of a bigger picture we choose to ignore. The most obvious symptom of this is that the only accepted form of causality is a time-based one. For most of us it is almost inconceivable that there could be any other mechanism linking events. However, such a connecting principle does seem possible. It has been described as acausal reality and formed an important part of Carl Jung's work. His book (5)"Synchronicity" is all about this. In it he attempts to explain events or confluences of events which are not explained by our classical notions of cause and effect, and appear to function in contradiction with our time-based reality. A good example is when you think of someone and almost immediately that person calls you. Another might be strange coincidences, such as meeting a friend in a most unlikely place or dreaming of something which happens shortly afterwards. My wife had an extremely strong experience of this when some weeks before the horrific fire in the King's Cross Underground station fire in London in the 1990s, she had a dream of just such an event. She was totally traumatised by it and when she read about the fire a little time after, her initial reaction was "my god this actually happened!".

We are all aware of this aspect of the world, and the fact that so many people consult healers, psychics, and astrologers to name but a few, is a testament to the fact that many people accept it, even if they don't understand it. It is a world which most of us tacitly admit exists but is pigeonholed under the heading "irrational and unexplainable". It is so at odds with our ordinary reality that we don't even try to understand it. However, this does not stop some very rational human beings taking advantage of it if happens to suit them. A good example is the use of divining to find water, oil or anything else. Apparently, there are those who can even divine from maps! This is something with no logical explanation and where the substance to be mapped is at a geographical distance. In a sense the time and distance between the diviner and what they find appears to disappear. All these phenomena are examples of this acausal reality peeking up above the parapet. As with alternative medicine, because they can be viewed as so threatening to our conventional reality there are many "rationalists" who attack them as unscientific hocus pocus.

So, it seems that our "reality" may not be quite as real as we think. Time which we all accept without question is clearly crucial and as I have already pointed out, we are prepared to brush aside all kinds of anomalies in order to avoid questioning its validity. The most obvious of these is its elasticity, the fact that we all experience change at different rates. This can manifest itself in extreme ways. I had a near death experience whilst tobogganing in the Alps. From the moment that I span out of control to the time when I came to a painful shuddering stop could only have been a few seconds at most, yet to me it felt like an eternity. It literally seems as though time goes into slow motion. I have heard about this kind of experience many times, almost always in a situation of extreme stress. Of course, a classic reply to this might be "Yes, it is true that we all experience the passage of time differently, in fact we all experience everything differently, but that does not in any way negate the fact that time exists". If the only argument I had against the existence of time was its elasticity, then I might be prepared to accept this. However, whilst it is true that people experience things in different ways, it is very unlikely that the differences can be as extreme as those with time. The differences are not just between different people but more importantly between different moments in people's lives. The passage of time can be looked at in the same way as the speed one travels at and it is unlikely that someone will experience travelling at the same speed in a car so differently on subsequent occasions that at one time the car will appear to be almost at a standstill, whilst at another it will seem to be going at a thousand miles an hour.

In order to create the regular unfolding of time that we all depend on, we have observed and memorised the dynamic patterns of change in our world, such as the movement of the Earth around the sun and the moon around the Earth, and extrapolated from that our world changes at an even rate. It is only because of our memory and our ability to imagine the future that we have been able to do this. These observations have been hugely important to us in that they have allowed us to plan for the future and it has been a great success. It has not therefore been a very difficult leap for us to believe that the rate of change exhibited by these repeating patterns is universal and constant. What we

I. TIME AND SPACE

have actually done is built a view of the world that suits our situation, whether it is by creating time, an absolute up and down, or a God. It is very interesting to me that it is science itself, the bedrock of our view of reality, that is itself discovering its limits and incongruities.

Although I don't for a minute believe that humans consciously decided to create time, its existence is the keystone of the way we perceive ourselves. I am no specialist in animal behaviour, yet it seems to me that the principal difference between humans and animals is that animals are not conscious of themselves as separate beings. That does not mean that they do not behave as individuals but rather that they are not aware of that difference. They simply behave in their own unique way. Humans on the other hand are from very early on in their lives aware of themselves being separate. Although the distinction I am making is a subtle one, it is absolutely vital in understanding what makes human behaviour different. Our concept of time plays an absolutely essential role in this. In order to have a true sense of being separate, it is essential to be able to imagine ourselves out of our current situation. We have to have an idea of ourselves in our head which we can place in a different place and time. When I decide that I will meet someone at a particular time tomorrow, I have to be able to believe that I am an independent being who is able to decide of his own free will how to behave and move around, not in the immediate present I am now in but in the greater world which includes future time and future places. I also need to be able to refer back to the past and have an awareness of everything that is not me. Being able to think this way involves a long and often painful apprenticeship which we all go through as babies and children. How successfully we go through it seems to have a bearing on how well we function in our society. Learning that we are not the world, but rather a being with limits that needs to respect other beings, is for us a huge and complicated task because our world is so much bigger than those of animals. This is because through the existence of time, in conjunction with the other dimensions, we have been able to create an enormously complex and vast world which can be very difficult to live in.

They are a hidden and completely ingrained part of human culture even if different peoples have a more or less rigid perception of their importance. The most obvious mechanism for this shared reality is speech. With language comes shared assumptions, shared beliefs and most importantly a shared view of reality. The moment we are able to perceive ourselves as being separate from our environment, other members of our social group also have to have similar notions, otherwise we will be alone in our world. Languages are in fact a perfect example of how we have divided up our future and past. I have recently become reacquainted with the theoretical bases of languages partly through my children and partly through learning a foreign language. What struck me as fascinating with regard to my young children is that their teachers have to explain to them how we view our world in order to explain the

I. TIME AND SPACE

grammar that underlies our languages. For example, the different tenses are based on different aspects of past, future or present life. You have the simple present, the past that has happened, the past that is happening, things that will happen in the future and others that might happen. I am currently in the process of learning Italian and even though the concepts of past and future etc are already engrained in me, I have to go through a very complex learning process in order to integrate the new language into my framework. In order for the new language to make sense to me, I have to understand how it deals with particular time-orientated situations, which will inevitably vary in certain cases from my native tongue. Until this becomes automated, I will find it difficult to express myself fluently in Italian and furthermore am likely to misunderstand what other people are saying.

In a sense our language actually dictates how we perceive our world. Language not only allows us to communicate among ourselves but helps create the common framework in which we live. An example of how these shared assumptions work would be when in our minds we imagine where we are going sometime in the future. If I tell my wife that I will be going to a conference on the other side of the world in six months' time, she will understand and accept what I say. She will in general not look at me as though I am mad! We both have a concept of geography and time and are therefore able to communicate about it. Yet when you begin to break down those concepts into their constituent parts, they begin to make much less sense. The idea of six months, which we are both so happy to accept, is actually totally meaningless if taken on its own. As I have already pointed out, we all experience the passage of time differently and neither of us have any idea what those six months will bring nor even if I will be alive then. What we are actually doing is unconsciously using conventions which enable us to believe that we are individuals with free choice. I have decided to go to Japan in six months' time for a conference and I have not only used language to imagine this but have also used it to communicate this plan to my wife. Of course, language is not the creator of this situation but merely the mechanism by which the framework we all accept as reality becomes universal. Human beings are genetically predetermined to speak, meaning that language is a natural part of our makeup. It has been superbly moulded so as to enable us to share our view of reality with our fellow human beings. The fact that this reality is anchored in language means that it is accepted as the reality because everyone who uses that language shares the same assumptions.

Language is an incredibly powerful and subtle mechanism for creating the illusion of a time-based reality. The reason for this is that it is based on abstraction. For example, if I use the word tree, what is in my head is an abstract idea of trees in general, rather than an idea of a specific tree at a specific time. This way I am able to communicate with other people and they will have an idea of what I am talking about. Language

I. TIME AND SPACE

uses the same mechanism for everything it describes. It creates a fixed abstraction which we all learn to accept as a meaningful representation of something that has been taken out of its context. If we come back to the example of trees, in nature it is clear that a tree does not exist out of its environment, yet through language we are able to have a concept of trees in general totally divorced from their environments. This perception is totally at odds with life as it actually unfolds minute by minute, yet appears to us to be completely real. Animals too use language albeit in a much more limited way and they too must use abstraction in order for it to work. When I talk to my dog about his ball, he is thinking about balls in general and not a specific ball at a specific time. However, the difference is that we humans have developed language to an extent where it totally dominates our lives. It is language that has cemented our notions of the past and the future. It is language that has enabled us to create the vast and complex world that is human society, in which we can imagine all kinds of situations, objects, people, and places which have no connection with our immediate situation. Its impact is so powerful that in general we are not even aware that it is there at all, it is simply an innate part of our existence. Of course, we realise that a lack of language poses a major problem. If for whatever reason we are unable to use language, we are totally isolated from society and life becomes well-nigh impossible. This is obviously the case for those that are deaf and dumb and, in their case, a huge effort has been made to find alternative means of communication. Given this, it is strange that we are so unaware of how the existence and use of language is so vital to the way our society functions.

In order to be able to make sense, language has to be based on abstracted snapshots of life and is never able to truly represent anything accurately. I have already used the example of a tree, and this same situation is repeated throughout all languages everywhere. The reason is that everything changes with the passage of time, yet language is unable to take this into account. Even if we take names which can be used to identify specific objects or people, and are therefore much less abstract than the words used to describe objects in general, the same problem applies. If for example I talk about a specific object such as Michelangelo's "David", the process still involves abstraction. This is because the statue of "David" is in reality different from moment to moment. Of course, the rate of change is incredibly slow because it was carved out of marble, and as such is not going to be directly perceivable by the human eye. However, this does not alter the fact that the David that I saw a month ago is not the same David that I saw 30 years ago. If you take living beings, this becomes much more obvious. Over 30 years it is perfectly obvious that someone has changed considerably. Yet language does not take this into account and in a sense is unable to. If it was forced to express every minute change in everything it described, it would very quickly become much too complex and incomprehensible. Language has to use abstraction in order for us to make sense of our world. By its very nature it ossifies and

I. TIME AND SPACE

artificially separates and, in this way, reflects how we actually function in relation to the world around us. As I have already mentioned, we need to make sense of our world in order to be able to live and thrive in it. If I am wandering around in the African bush on foot and I see a lion, I will immediately be afraid and take action to try and neutralise that perceived threat, in one way or other. What is not going to help the situation is simply observing the lion as a completely unique creature with no connection to any other lion. In doing so I may be observing life more openly and with less preconceptions, but the result is that I am likely to get eaten! This comes back to what I was saying before about using memories of past events to improve one's ability to survive. In order for this to function effectively you need to use abstraction. It's not much use if my dog once he has been hit by a car, only seeks to avoid the car that once hit him. If he is going to successfully avoid further injury from cars, he needs to avoid cars in general. If I wish to avoid getting eaten by a lion, I need to perceive the lion in an abstracted form and thus react appropriately to threat.

It should therefore be becoming clear that the abstraction of language is one of the foundations upon which our life on Earth is based. Yet as I have already pointed out, humans do not behave in the same way as other life forms. So, in what way does the use of language make us different to other living beings? Yes, living beings in general use abstraction in association with memory in order to function more successfully on

Earth, but with language we have taken this process to a completely new level. We are not making sense of the world around us, but rather creating an entirely new world which often has almost no connection to our immediate environment at all. This is of course the world of ideas, which as I have already explained requires a concept of a past, a future and a here and there. We need language for this world to function and appear real. I can't touch the past or the future, so I need another tool with which to describe it. I need a tool which other people can understand, and which will enable me to appear coherent. Language, because it is universal and genetically pre-determined, acts as the cement which makes our illusory time-based world real. This process has been gradually going on since the beginnings of human life on Earth with our time-based world becoming ever more complex, sophisticated and universal. Of course, there have always been innumerable languages and dialects in the world which are all associated with distinct outlooks. Clearly a hunter gatherer and a born and bred Londoner are going to have a different perception of reality. This will clearly make communication more challenging, and both will find it difficult to live in the other's world. However, this doesn't alter the fact that hunter gatherers as much as Londoners have an awareness of themselves as independent beings that can move around in time and space. Their language makes their version of reality, function in their community. It could be argued that 'modern man' has developed and expanded this illusory world and it is clear that with globalisation and the development of English as a global language, there are now huge numbers of people who share the same reality. Furthermore, many languages are based on similar concepts even if the actual symbols and underlying structures are different.

It is this separation from our immediate environment personified in our individuality, which is both essential to our success and at the root of our suffering. This is not only dependent on our perception of time but also the three dimensions. This can be summed up in the concept of the space-time continuum which, although widely accepted in physics, is not really understood in wider society. Yet it is only by understanding how we live our lives in relation to space-time that we can begin to see how our perception of the world makes our suffering inevitable.

Although in the realm of physics time is now accepted as the fourth dimension, in everyday life the three dimensions are perceived to exist independently. On the one hand we have our physical world which we believe remains generally fixed, and on the other hand we have ourselves who move around in it using time as a measure. For example, when we decide that we are going to go somewhere at a certain time, the somewhere exists solidly in its three dimensions, and time is the measure which allows us to calculate when in the geography of our lives we will get there. When we describe physical objects, we also base it on three dimensions, and this involves an implicit acceptance that those objects are not in the process of changing.

What is strange about this is that we forget that without time the three dimensions make no sense at all. For example, if you are describing a place where you have been you need to make it clear when that was. Paris in 1976 is not the same place as Paris in 2011. The moment you add time to the equation it all becomes a lot clearer. When you think about this it is completely obvious and we do of course use time and space together in order to locate ourselves in this world. However, this does not alter the fact that we view them as separate. The interesting question is why. It comes back to the very same points that I have already raised about how animals use memorisation and categorisation in order to survive in this world. We have to categorise in order for our memorisation to be useful. If I wish to learn from what I have done in order to improve my ability to survive on Earth, I need to be able to use the memory of previous events to help me in the future. For this to work my brain has to latch on to the common features of beings, environmental features, events etc. and ignore the fact that nothing is ever really the same. If by accident you learn that a particular plant is good to eat, you need to be able to realise that you can also eat other examples of the same species. If you simply memorised that particular plant at that particular time, you would never find another one and you would not have learnt anything at all. It is essential for us to

I. TIME AND SPACE

abstract the world around us into categories and in doing so we inadvertently separate time from space.

This becomes even more important when, as we humans have done, you start to develop a sense of self-awareness. Simply to have a notion of your self requires abstraction. If we were unable to abstract ourselves out of our particular situation in the space-time continuum there is no way that we could conceive of ourselves as individuals. In practical terms it is simply not possible to live in the world as it really is. Strictly speaking, everything is unique because everything changes all of the time, and it is just not possible to take a snapshot of something and then say that that snapshot is the something because by the time you have taken the snapshot everything has already changed. Whilst it is possible to understand this from a philosophical and scientific perspective, it would be impossible to live our day-to-day lives in this way. Our memories would be completely useless as nothing that we remembered from before would ever exist again and it would therefore be totally impossible to adapt and learn from our environment. We would simply not be able to progress at all and my guess is that any living being that functioned this way would not last very long! As I have already said, all sentient beings use memory to help them adapt and thrive in this world. So, it seems that the abstraction and categorisation of our world is an essential and integral part of our functioning. It is in fact at the very root of our approach to life. With the development of self-awareness this process has developed more and more to a point where we have created a totally alternative world which seems to bear almost no relation to actual reality at all. We have not only categorised and abstracted the immediate environment, but by being able to imagine ourselves as separate to other people and the world around us, we have created a completely new world of the past and future, here and there.

In this world space plays just as an important role as time. Just in the same way that we need time to locate ourselves in relation to others, the same applies to the three dimensions of space. There is not much use organising to meet someone at a certain time if you don't specify where! Time and space only work when used together. Yet just as our notions of time are completely artificial, the same applies for space. The problem here, as with time alone, is perception. I am not denying that our world exists or that it changes, but am simply saying that we have created measuring sticks to make sense of how we perceive it. If we truly lived the space-time continuum as described in physics, life would be impossible. We wouldn't have a universal concept of time as we would be aware of it speeding up and slowing down depending on our speed and the gravitational fields. We would not be able to have a concept of the future or anywhere else, as we would be aware that we were completely linked to our environment, which itself was in a process of continual change. We would be unable to abstract anything, meaning we would be unable to imagine anything out of its context. The world would be one giant dynamic changing reality in which everything was relative to everything else. It is, in effect, impossible to imagine such a world as we could not survive in it at all. We have to separate time from space and ourselves from our world if we wish to thrive as we have done. It comes back to what Carlo Rovelli, the Italian Astro-physicist said about time, absolute simultaneity and an absolute up and down, being features of the small garden that makes up our world. Science and philosophy might prove that this small world is not logical, but it doesn't make our world any less real to us. Even ideas such as gravity that are widely accepted don't really affect our lives very much. As far as our daily lives are concerned, objects weigh something and that is all that matters to us. The fact that in outer space a person who weighs 200kg would be weightless is unlikely to cheer them up very much. All that matters to us is what is relevant to us in our daily lives, and our classical notions of space work very well.

However, as Carlo Rovelli has already worked out with regard to time, when you begin to dig beneath the surface you can see that our perception of space is actually just a mirage. A good example of this is when we think or talk about a country. This is something we do all the time without paying the slightest bit of attention to what we actually mean. If you watch the news on the television, there are frequent references to places. An example might be: X number of soldiers were killed and injured today in Afghanistan. We all just accept this whilst thinking how absolutely awful it is and quite probably thinking of those soldiers' families and what they must being going through. Almost no one will ever give a thought to the fact that this information, when you begin to dig beneath the surface, makes absolutely no sense at all. Firstly, what exactly is meant by Afghanistan? In talking about a country in this way you are relying on a huge number of shared assumptions which when you actually analyse them don't add up at all. The easiest way to do this is to use the space-time continuum as a measuring stick. You then realise that Afghanistan is just like any other label which is used to describe a shared concept. Outside our shared human reality there is no such thing as Afghanistan, because there is no one fixed experience which can define it. Every single person, even though they might be happy to accept the term without questioning, will have a different idea of what they mean by it. Most TV viewers watching the news on a regular basis will associate Afghanistan with death and destruction. They might also have pictures in their head related to TV footage they have seen, again mostly of a negative nature. However, for someone who had been born and brought up there, they might well have very positive memories related to their childhood. Memories of their family, their village or town and of their friends. To a geographer, Afghanistan will mean size, topography, population, demographics, climate, economy and the many other measures which make up their description of a country. The fact that no two people have the same idea of what Afghanistan is does

I. TIME AND SPACE

not, however, stop them understanding what is being talked about when it is mentioned. What I am trying to say is that there is not one definitive picture of Afghanistan or anywhere else. What appears to us straightforward and obvious is in fact nebulous and uncertain, and in a general sense entirely meaningless. Although in the case of the news it really doesn't matter if it makes sense or not, the reason we accept what they say without question is that this way of looking at things is essential to our daily lives. When we decide to go somewhere, we take the necessary measures such as getting in our car and driving in the right direction. We might need to look at a map or punch the address into our GPS. However, in all cases the basic principles will be the same, as we will be doing something that is based on unquestioned shared assumptions. Our destination will have been fixed in time and space on a map and we all accept this abstraction as an accurate and relevant representation of where we believe we are going. However, it is only because in general things change slowly that such an approach is possible, and if the process of change speeds up, we can quickly become disorientated. After a major natural disaster such as a flood or an earthquake, a place can quickly become unrecognisable. It is at this point that it becomes obvious that our concept of place is artificial as the place in question no longer bears any resemblance to the abstract notion we had of it. However, even in less dramatic circumstances it is clear that our idea of somewhere is actually just that: an idea. For example, what do you think of when you imagine Paris, London or New York? If you have never visited Paris, you might have a vision of the Eiffel Tower which you have seen on television or on a postcard. That is probably the reason that cities like to have symbols, so that they can be easily differentiated visually from other places. But for someone who has visited Paris or lived there, mention of the city will bring up a completely different picture. It will relate to that person's experiences there. If they own a property, it could be their house, or it could be an emotional feeling. If someone has had a bad experience somewhere, emotions related to that bad experience could be felt. A striking example for me is South Africa. I managed to get an extremely bad case of malaria when I was there on honeymoon! If someone mentions South Africa to me today, my overriding reaction is a memory of feeling absolutely horrible. Of course, the opposite is equally possible. Many people have very happy associations with places. Maybe somewhere they used to go on holiday or a childhood home. If they happen to hear that place mentioned, it will immediately bring back happy memories. However, those memories will have little relevance to anyone else and there may not even be much physical resemblance between how they see the place in their head and how it looks today. Even when we talk about a city, the mental images which we have in our head which represent it will be different to other people's. This is as much the case for people who are in the place as for those who imagine it from afar. The only experience which can in any sense be described as real is the one we are having right now. Yet if we actually thought this way in our

I. TIME AND SPACE

daily lives, we would never actually go anywhere or get anything done. If for my job I am told that I need to go to Berlin next week, it would cause real problems if I turned around to my boss and told him that Berlin doesn't actually exist and that as a result it is totally illogical to plan to go there. The best result is that I would get the sack, and the worst is that I would get packed off to a lunatic asylum. We all accept that places exist independently of space-time and we need to do so in order to live our lives. Yet by doing so we are placing ourselves in contradiction with the way the universe actually functions, and although we are mostly unable to see this, we are affected by it. The world of three dimensions that we live in is a solid unchanging world full of certainty, backed up by facts and figures. It is the world of bricks and mortar, maps, explored and named landscapes, countries, cities, languages and daily news. It is a world in which we feel comfortable because we can rely on it to provide us with the parameters, we need to feel secure. Yet paradoxically enough it actually achieves quite the opposite of what we hope for. The reason for this is, as I have already mentioned, because this certain, fixed solid world is in direct conflict with life as it actually unfolds. That is to say that our belief in this Cartesian world sits in direct contrast to our daily experiences. We all experience change on a daily basis, and from time to time are faced with rapid and irreversible alterations to our lives. There are innumerable examples of this with obvious ones being sudden illnesses and bereavements. However, almost any sudden change can seriously destabilise people.

Obviously, we all react differently to such events and some people are much more resilient than others. From my perspective the most important point is that this is a universal phenomenon which is an inevitable part of the way we live on Earth. Our happiness, however you choose to define it, is a highly fragile thing because we are so vulnerable to the unexpected twists and turns that life throws at us. It is during these moments of extreme change that we are brought face to face with the actual reality of life. In this reality nothing is permanent, nothing is fixed and the foundations which we have based our lives on can be swept away in minutes. The obvious examples are the dramatic events which fill our headlines on a regular basis. The wars, famines, accidents, earthquakes, floods, and the myriad other dramatic and often deadly events that can destroy our world. If our difficulty with this state of affairs was simply restricted to major disasters, most of us would find life quite easy to cope with. Yet what is interesting is that it is not only extreme events which can unsettle us. Often people are just aware that something is not quite right in their lives. This can be triggered by a multitude of different factors such as suddenly noticing that we are older or that we no longer attract the opposite sex in the way we used to. It could be waking up one day and realising that you hate your job and are bored of your friends and where you live. The reasons and potential scenarios are endless, and I am sure that almost everyone can think of examples in their own lives. These are moments when the façade of our illusory world starts to crack, and we begin to question its validity.

If all of this sounds crazy it is only because I am busy pulling the foundations of your lives from under your feet! If neither time nor space exist as separate realities, then the world which we all accept as real and which we live in on a day-to-day basis is actually all an illusion. This does not mean that the physical world does not exist, but rather that our perception of it, is just that: a perception. When you and everyone around you looks at the world in the same way, it is almost impossible to imagine that this totally normal way of looking at things could be illusory. Of course, I am not the first person to have spoken about this. For thousands of years Buddhists and Taoists have challenged the classical view of reality and have identified it as the source of suffering. For some Zen Buddhists, our normal view of the world is actually viewed as heresy. By this they are not saying that you have said or done something so offensive to the doctrine of their religion that you should be declared a heretic, but rather that it is heretical to live an illusion and that the true path is experiencing life as it is and not as we believe it to be. To many of us this sounds completely crazy. Life is as it appears to us and the idea that it could be an illusion is absurd. Yet if you examine our world carefully, you can, as I have been explaining, begin to see the foundations upon which it is built. This is not something which is easy to do, as we are genetically programmed and educated to accept this reality as the only valid one.

So, we live in an invented world which oddly enough is divorced from our environment and the dynamic process of change which underlies the universe. This has involved the creation of an artificial spatial world, with time as a separate measuring principle, where we can place ourselves. So where is this world? It does not physically exist, and consequently can only exist in our minds. But it is not enough for it to exist in only one person's mind, for when that happens they are quickly described as mad and sent off for treatment! It has to exist in enough people's minds for it to become a shared reality. What is interesting is that this shared reality is made up of the slowly acquired knowledge that makes up the human world. It is knowledge that is deeply ingrained in the human psyche and that starts being taught to us from the moment we are born. It is, as I have already mentioned, an essential feature of languages, and other forms of communication such as gestures, expressions etc. This reality, even though it varies hugely according to our culture, nationality, belief system etc., is in its basic parameters common to all humankind. All human cultures share many basic concepts, the most fundamental one being that we exist as independent entities. This necessitates being able to move around in spaces and times separate from our immediate environment. In its most basic form this will involve shared memories of places other than where we are right now. An example might be some members of an ancient tribe, agreeing to meet at a particular tree which everyone knows about. To everyone within that tribe, the tree exists and they would know how to get

I. TIME AND SPACE

there. They might even be able to explain to a fellow tribesman how to find it, by using other commonly known reference points. In their world they had no maps, no coordinates, no compasses or GPS, and no clocks, and yet were very able to communicate to each other about their physical world. Even tribes who did not share the same language, traditions or knowledge of their environment, would have shared the same basic approach to life. An approach which necessitated living in a world beyond their immediate environment, which enabled them to believe that they existed as individuals and were able to move around in an illusory world which they shared a common belief in.

However, as society has become more sophisticated, and we have needed to create more widely accepted criteria for describing our environment, we have divided up our physical world with distances and coordinates. This process has been gradually accelerating as human civilisation has advanced. Five hundred years ago a map was a rare and very valuable item, but as time has passed mapping has become ever more universal and available. Today it has reached a point where at the touch of a button we are able to see maps of almost anywhere on Earth. When we drive around in our cars, we use GPS systems which not only have very detailed maps of where we are driving but are even able to tell us where we are and where we should go. This has required incredibly detailed mapping, which has little by little expanded the known world and yet paradoxically made it smaller. Areas which have not yet been mapped are generally described as undiscovered. The place itself of course is completely unaware of the process and not in the least bit interested! One of the effects of mapping is to fix the mapped area in time as well as space and from the point of view of the person looking at the map, the place is completely static. This is quite similar to the way the body is viewed in anatomy, i.e. as a collection of static parts. The moment we create a symbol to represent something or somewhere, we are abstracting it and it cannot be an accurate representation at all. In reality, a body is living, dynamic and in a constant state of movement and change. The same is true of places which are always changing due to the weather, the state of the vegetation or the temperature to give just a few examples. I live in the mountains and here the landscape is subject to extreme changes. The mountains in the winter bear almost no relation to the mountains in the summer. The actual shapes of the mountains change, not only between summer and winter but whenever it snows or warms up. Streams disappear, waterfalls are frozen, and tracks and roads are covered over. As the seasons change and with the variations in weather patterns, my environment alters in a radical way. One can see from this, that just like a human being, a mountain is in a constant state of change. However, it would simply not be practical to change the name of a mountain every millisecond of its existence. The fact that nothing is the same from moment to moment has to be ignored, otherwise we would not be able to make any sense of our environment. We have to create an abstracted notion of that mountain so that we can

I. TIME AND SPACE

all share our concept of it. Such notions are in fact symbols. The use of symbols is at the very basis of our functioning. Language relies on this absolutely in order to be able to work. Anything that is named by language is a symbol. For example, when you talk about a dog, you have an idea of what it means; however, it is obvious that not only are all dogs different but furthermore no individual dog is the same in one moment as in the next. Language uses symbols or fixed abstractions for absolutely everything which it describes and as I have already mentioned is the principal mechanism by which shared perceptions of the world become socially anchored.

In order for our illusory world to make sense we have gradually broken down its function into millions of constituent parts and have used language and numbers as the mechanism for sharing this. The dominant theme is the process of separation and labelling. As I have already mentioned, a striking example of this is the human body, which in a sense can be considered our primary space. Its gradual exploration was an extremely important part of the Renaissance and its humanist principles. This process accelerated during the enlightenment, when dissection became widespread. We have now named almost every known constituent part and worked out the functioning of many of its systems. However, this approach is based on the same illusory reality as the rest of our lives. Body parts simply don't have a life of their own, nor do they think of themselves as being separate to the rest of the body or the rest of the universe! We have, as with everything else, abstracted the parts of the body from the whole and given them symbols to represent them by which we then imagine as being real. Yet the irony is that not only do body parts only make sense in the context of the body, but furthermore no body part is actually the same from moment to moment. What we are of course doing is abstracting the common features of say a heart and using this to create a commonly accepted perception of it. This allows us to talk about hearts in general and it allows branches of medicine to specialise in the treatment of heart problems. As with all our other technological and medical advances, this approach appears to work. We are able to treat almost all diseases, repair extraordinary injuries and even transplant body parts from one person to another!

Paradoxically, on the one hand our world which is based on a belief in cause and effect functions incredibly well, yet on the other hand we all feel terribly insecure because we know that we don't really exist in the way our rational Cartesian world would have us believe. This contradiction is at the root of the human condition, yet appears to be something that we are unaware of at least on a conscious level. We accept without question the enormously complex world of the past, the future, the here and the there, and cannot see that it is completely unrelated to the actual reality which unfolds in a constant present. As a consequence, we are often living completely in our heads, totally unaware of what is going on around us. Even if we are aware, that

I. TIME AND SPACE

awareness is completely conditioned by our past and our genetic inheritance. To give an example, if you look at a book, in your head you automatically know what it is. When you look at the writing on the cover, you are able to read what it says and have a notion of the type of book it is. You are therefore looking at it through the lens of conditioning. This may seem illogical, but this is only the case because our conditioning is so strong that it seems natural to us. If you were able to look at an object or even some writing free from conditioning, it would not have any meaning for you at all. The writing would just appear to be a series of lines and squiggles with no significance at all. Every situation we are in, everything we look at, feel, smell, hear or sense is subject to our interpretation. In fact, our brain is permanently interpreting the world for us. When we look, hear, feel, touch or hear anything, we are busy interpreting it. If we don't immediately understand what it is we have come across, our brains will do their best to interpret it for us. If we have never come across something before, it will often leave us totally disorientated and this is generally an uncomfortable feeling for us. An example of this type of feeling is when you wake up in an unfamiliar place, a hotel room or another person's house, it can often take a few minutes to work out where we are. During this period, we can feel completely disorientated and at sea. In general, if we can't work out where we are or what is going on, we are not very happy. We need to be able to make sense of our immediate world in order to feel comfortable, and in order to make sense of it we need to be able to perceive our surroundings in relation to knowledge we have acquired or been taught.

Of course, the precise interpretation will be different from person to person and from social group to social group. The more in common people have, the closer their perception of the world will be and the easier it will be for them to communicate. The reverse is always true, which is why relations between peoples of different cultures are very open to misunderstandings. It is always just a question of degree as no two people have exactly the same perception of the world. These misunderstandings tend to accentuate our sense of insecurity, which originates from our illusory individuality. It is extremely common to mistakenly assume that someone else's behaviour is related to us. You might, for example, be upset by the behaviour of a work colleague and think that you have done something to offend them. However, quite frequently their behaviour has absolutely nothing to do with you but is being caused by something completely unrelated. In fact, we constantly misunderstand each other and misinterpret each other's actions. This is one of the main obstacles we face in relationships and it is, for the reasons I have already mentioned, inevitable. We always interpret everything in relation to ourselves because our egos feel constantly under threat. We endlessly seek affirmation of our importance because if we are important, we must exist. Thus, it is extremely difficult for us to believe that someone else's behaviour has nothing to do with us at all. Even if intellectually

I. TIME AND SPACE

we know this to be true, from an emotional level it is a challenge to accept it.

Because the world we base our notion of individuality on is an invented one, there will be enormous variations in what makes it up. Yes, the basic parameters are the same in that everyone believes that they have lives independent of their environment, although the contents of this artificial world will vary greatly. The customs, habits and belief systems all vary enormously and because they play an important role in establishing identity, can easily lead to misunderstandings and often conflict. We are always looking for differences in order to identify ourselves and this process inevitably leads us to see ourselves in relation to others. In a sense we need the other in order to define ourselves and this is why we often feel in competition with those around us. Of course, emotions such as jealousy are not confined to human beings as anyone who owns a dog well knows, but because our situation is so much more fragile than that of animals, and our ability to act so much greater, its impact is likely to be more significant for us and others. This explains how we can come to hate and even injure and kill people who have not done anything to us at all. It is perfectly obvious that in the vast majority of cases, human unpleasantness towards others is not caused by the victims. Even if you take a simple work or school situation, where someone is being bullied, they have almost never "done" anything nasty to their persecutors. Yes, they might have some character and/or physical traits that make them more likely to be bullied than others, but this is totally different to having done anything to deserve it. The bullies are picking on others in order to boost their own sense of self-importance. This is a way for them to affirm their existence in the face of change and uncertainty. It is often said that it is those who are insecure that make the worst bullies and this makes a lot of sense to me. There are obviously character traits which are necessary for this type of behaviour, but this does not alter the fundamental point. It is because our sense of self or ego is constantly put into question that we seek ways to bolster it.

The only human beings who avoid this trap are infants or the few lucky enlightened ones (if they actually exist!). Young children are like an unprogrammed computer. All the hardware which is needed to allow them to develop into social beings is present, but the software is not installed yet. The hardware is their genetic inheritance. A child is genetically programmed to be able to develop conscious thought, including a sense of the past and the future, and all the other mental and emotional skills required to function in human society. However, until the software is installed, they cannot see the future, they cannot distinguish themselves from others, in fact they are not even aware that they exist. They react immediately and instinctively to their surroundings. They exist in an eternal present, feeling and reacting directly to the environment around them and their own sensory perceptions. As they grow up and are gradually socialised, this begins to change. They begin to develop an idea of where they stop, and the

I. TIME AND SPACE

rest of the world begins. They begin to have a concept of the past and the future and of here and there. Slowly a direct experience of life is replaced by our conditioned and illusory one. Of course, this appears to be a natural process as we are inherently predisposed to this type of development. In essence, it is more or less inevitable that we end up this way. This pattern of separation has enabled human beings to be hugely successful, as it is our ability to calculate, plan, organise and learn from our mistakes which has allowed us to get where we are today. It is often said that we are the most dangerous predator, and it is not our strength which has made us so but our intelligence. Yet paradoxically enough, this very same intelligence is the cause of our suffering.

So we live and believe in a world with very shaky foundations, which only exists because we have a shared perception of its function, rooted in our genetic origins and our environmental upbringing. This world is in conflict with the underlying reality of life, which is a continuous unfolding present, oblivious to the future, past and spatial orientation. In this underlying reality there is no place for individuality as we know it. We simply do not exist as separate beings in the way we imagine it, that is with an independent existence able to move around in time and the three spatial dimensions. All of this exists solely in our minds. It is a completely mind-blowing and of course paradoxical situation for it is only by perceiving the world in this way that we have been able to develop as we have done. I would not be able to have the thoughts I am having or write this book if I did not live my life as though I was an independent being. All of human civilisation, including our achievements in art, music, literature, science and technology are dependent on it. Yet this does not in any way alter the fact that our reality is a delusion, and that this delusion is at the very root our suffering.

Carlo Rovelli- Beyond time
Einstein- Letter to friend Bello
Einstein_ Quote vs. quantum mechanics

2. THE INDIVIDUAL

The idea of individuality is completely natural to us. It is as fundamental an aspect of our existence as time, space and gravity. We all have characters, physical aspects and histories which differentiate us from everyone else. In a sense, it is possible to say that our individuality is our existence, and it is not something that we generally question. Yet what exactly do we mean when we talk about an individual or even individuality? Are we talking about the physical and character traits that define us? Or are we referring to the legal status that gives us all a place in society with its associated duties and rights? These are not questions that we ask ourselves very often if at all, yet what may on the surface seem perfectly obvious is, when you begin to scratch a little below the surface, much less clear cut than we could ever imagine.

We base our assumptions on the fact that individuality is something fixed and easily identifiable, and from an administrative perspective we are regarded as the same person from birth until death. If instead, we were viewed as a different person after every minute change we experienced, the system would collapse in minutes! In the case of our legal identity, the parameters are relatively few, i.e. our name, gender, date and place of birth and nationality. In a sense we are abstracted into parameters which are unchangeable (or are rarely changed) and are therefore relatively easily classified. However, if we begin to consider identity in a more general sense, the potential parameters are simply endless and furthermore often highly changeable. Our social background, ethnic mix, religion, age, dress style, job or role in society, weight, and physical attractiveness are just a few of these characteristics. They interact in a constantly evolving and dynamic process which produces our identity on a moment-by-moment basis. Even the apparently fixed aspects are subjected to different interpretations at different moments of our lives. We might feel comfortable in our social class at one point in our lives, yet later perhaps because our financial situation has evolved, we see that very same social class as an embarrassment.

Yet we are generally happy to talk about the characteristics of the people we know as being permanent ones. If someone is described as rich and good looking, we do not imagine these aspects of their being as likely to change. The same can be said for character traits such as kindness or meanness. In fact, it is generally accepted that people don't change with a strong notion of individual identity

2. THE INDIVIDUAL

reflected in all aspects of society. For example, today's democratic systems are based on individual rights and responsibilities. It is individuals that are able to vote in elections, sit on juries or be elected as members of parliament. The rights enshrined in a charter such as the European bill of human rights are individual ones. It is about an individual's rights in relation to the state and society. Yet there is no need for the bill to start by defining what we mean by individuality. This is the case regardless of the type of belief system or society you live in. Whether you live in a socialist or capitalist country, a democracy or a dictatorship, and whether you are religious or an atheist, you all accept individuality as a de facto reality. Of course, there are anomalies and incongruities which come along and challenge that blind acceptance. However, what these tend to do is to make life difficult for us rather than lead us to question the concept of individuality itself.

A very contemporary example is when people change their sexual identity via sex change operations. Should the state accept this change or not? Is your sex defined biologically or psychologically? These are questions which tend to upset our traditional notions of identity and will often elicit very strong opinions from people. Another one is mental illness; at what point can someone be considered unable to make their own decisions? By taking away this aspect of their existence, they lose a part of what defines them, at the very least from a legal perspective. To get around this we simply reclassify them as "the mentally ill", meaning an individual who cannot be allowed to have the full rights that make up a "mentally competent" person. In both those cases that individual has undergone such a major change that his or her legal status has been altered. In neither case is the situation clear cut and in both there is endless room for disagreement.

These examples involve sudden or dramatic change, yet we know that we are constantly changing in all aspects of our being. Apparently, every cell in our body is completely replaced every seven years. However, this does not seem to stop us being convinced that the "real me" never changes. Recent advances in genetics with the mapping of the human genome at first appear to support this idea. We all have a genetic blueprint which we are born with and which defines our individuality. If this is the case then it is easy to believe that a permanent me, at least genetically, actually exists. However, even this cornerstone of our identity melts away when examined a little closer. The fact it is that the individual does not have a fixed and unchangeable blueprint which determines what they will be like throughout their lives. Although our genetic make-up is fixed at birth, how those genes actually function and express themselves is extremely changeable and is affected by an array of environmental factors. They are literately turned on, turned off, dimmed and brightened in a highly complex interactive and dynamic process. There is no you or me with fixed genetic destinies but rather a world of possibilities in which our genes act as guidelines. This is a process of constant change in

2. THE INDIVIDUAL

which the you of yesterday is simply not the same as the you of tomorrow. This does not mean that there are no differences between people, but rather that there are not only differences between people, but also between the same person at different times of his or her life. The same can, of course, be said for any living being or thing, and it is clear that this dynamic differentiation is an inescapable part of existence. However, what makes the human situation unique is the fact that an animal or a plant does not have a concept of its own individuality; it just does its thing. We might name it and give it an identity, but this will not be something which it will worry about!

As I have already discussed in the last chapter, our individuality is dependent on our belief in the four dimensions and our ability to move around in them independently of our immediate environment. This allows us to have an awareness of ourselves separate from our environment. However, the concept we have of ourselves is actually highly complex and fluid. Although we might believe that we are one person with a fixed identity based on physical and character traits, the reality is quite different. Our identity is actually based on how we see ourselves and this is in turn based on a multitude of different and highly variable factors. It is also likely to change depending on the situation we find ourselves in. For example, a man when he is at home with his children will not see himself in the same way as when he is at work dealing with colleagues or clients. To some extent we all have multiple personalities based on an endless array of racial, social, economic and religious identities which often cross over with each other. Our individuality does not exist independently of our world, but depends on our ideas of gender, race, social situation, immediate environment, age and many other physical, psychological and social characteristics.

An obvious example is our gender. It is a hugely important part of who we are and plays a major role in defining how we view ourselves. Gender, whether male or female, has characteristics which are widely accepted. As with an individual this will include both physical and character traits. If we take femininity as an example there exists a widely accepted idea of what being a woman is, as opposed to a man. Even though the idea of femininity has evolved over time and different women will have different perceptions of it, it exists as a universal concept. The fact that one person's idea of femininity may be completely different to another's, does not stop us accepting the idea of femininity in general. This is exactly the same process as any other kind of labelling, whether it is of countries, body parts or anything else. In reality, there is no such thing as male and female, as both these concepts are merely abstractions, which as with all other abstractions enable us to interpret and make sense of our world. Obviously, men and women are distinguished by their morphology and the functioning of certain aspects of their physiology; however, this would be of no consequence to our sense of self if we were not aware of it. What we have done is to take one of the naturally occurring

2. THE INDIVIDUAL

differentiators in nature and expanded it into our brave new space-time-based world. What before was simply a genetically-based determinant of our physical make-up and behaviour has become an essential building block in the construction which is our identity. So, when I say that gender is a social construction, what I am talking about is our idea of gender and how it relates to us. However, what is even more extraordinary about this process is that, unlike animals, we do not restrict ourselves to using abstraction to help us function and thrive in the natural world, but use abstract ideas, i.e. an idea without an actual physical reference point, in order to shore up our identity and sense of self. Thus, in the case of gender it is extremely important whether we regard ourselves as women or men, as it is an essential building block in the establishment of our identity. The gender we associate ourselves with has a whole array of features which we subscribe to. Just as with all the other abstract notions we use in our world, this process will be anchored in language and apparently commonly accepted notions. Of course, as with all other ideas this will vary from community to community and country to country; however, the basic process will be identical. Once a child is consciously aware of his (male) gender, and it becomes a vital part of what makes up his identity, he will begin to unconsciously assimilate the features which make it up. This is how you end up with typical male/female role playing. The downside of all this, as with all other features of our identity, is that if we do not manage to succeed in achieving the goals enshrined in our gender identity, our sense of self is threatened. Today we talk about how men's sense of self-worth is gradually being undermined, because they are no longer able to fully express their maleness. What is actually going on is that there is a gap between the ideas many men have of what being a man involves and what they are actually experiencing in their lives. The result is that their sense of identity and self-worth feels threatened. Society is changing but the shared assumptions which make up the male-female divide are clearly lagging behind. This is in fact a constant process as the dynamic and fluid nature of life is always showing up our need for rigid identities for what it is: an illusion. Our idea of gender is in reality a purely social construction, yet this is something which is very difficult for us to accept, whatever political or social beliefs you might have. We are led to believe that it is only conservative and reactionary forces which stick to traditional notions of gender identity, but this is not the case. The very idea of gender requires us to believe that an abstract idea is actually real.

So, for example, feminism would make no sense without the concept of women and men having distinct identities. Even if (as in this case) the purpose of feminism is to change commonly accepted notions and role playing, the basic process remains unchanged. Of course, male-female is only one of many differences, as our individuality is made up of a pastiche of shared identities. Yet as with our gender, none of these shared identities are carved in stone. Whether it is our nationality, age, social class, profession, wealth bracket,

2. THE INDIVIDUAL

ethnic group, educational background or anything else, everything is merely an abstraction or an idea, with no concrete basis. A good example is nationality, which on the surface seems to be an obvious and immutable fact. Whilst this may be the case from an administrative perspective, in other ways this is not the case at all. For example, being Japanese is something which is strongly defined by race, whilst being American is something which is defined far more by its culture and belief systems. So Japanese and Americans will not have the same idea of what nationality actually means, even though on the surface the idea would seem to be universal.

There are also always going to be innumerable subdivisions within an apparently homogenous identity. If you are an American you will view yourself very differently depending on your geographical origin, race, social class, gender etc. For example, there has for a long time been a big difference between the people of the North-east USA or the Yankees, and the people of the South. This type of difference exists in every country and can often apply to very small regions. Where I live in the French Alps, you are regarded as a foreigner unless you come from the actual village you live in. Even people in the next valley are not fully accepted as locals. In the modern world with the onset of "globalisation" such differences are maybe diminishing a little; however, they are still very much alive. As such, nationality is only one of the many geographically-based origins of identity. Depending on a multitude of factors which will vary with place and time, nationality may or may not be of particular importance. So, for example an Italian man, especially when he is in Italy, will generally be much more concerned about his local region such as Tuscany or Sicily, than his Italianness; however, during the football World Cup, especially if Italy is winning, his Italian nationality will suddenly take on a lot more importance! Nationality is of course nebulous in many other ways, as you may have one legal national identity and yet another emotional one. This may be the result of immigration or simply the fact that the country you identity yourself with, e.g. England or Scotland, is not a sovereign nation.

Another important aspect of our identity is social class. In some societies such as India, you are born into a social class and it is likely to have an impact on your life until you die. Although India is an extreme example, this pattern repeats itself to a greater or lesser degree all over the world. England is renowned for its class system and it is possible to recognise which class someone comes from the moment they open their mouth. However, just as with nationality, your class status is a lot more fluid and open to interpretation than we would believe. Many people change their social class within their lives, whilst some still feel that they belong to their original social group even if their circumstances have totally changed. You hear of quite a few people who have built large fortunes but continue to regard themselves as working class. Furthermore, the relevance of class changes with society, and this can

2. THE INDIVIDUAL

leave people feeling pretty confused. In many parts of the UK and the post-industrialised world, the industries which provided a basis for the existence of a working class have disappeared. Many of the people who lived and worked in those communities would have found those changes very difficult to cope with. In fact, it is extraordinary how people cling on to what they know and what they feel comfortable with. For example, Britain's coalminers fiercely resisted the gradual closing down of their industry. Of course, one can understand that people don't want to lose their jobs; however, the loss was more than just about jobs, but also about way of life. To many people it might seem surprising that you would want to cling on to a way of life based on a job that must have been very hard both physically and psychologically.

Another extremely important identifier in society is age. People of the same age tend to identify and socialise with each other. Children, adolescents, young adults, the middle aged, the list is endless. Of course, what is interesting about age in relation to most other aspects of identity is that it is constantly changing. The fact that we age is a serious challenge to those who believe, as most of us do, that there is an innate and unchanging essence to each of our existences. A lot of philosophy is devoted to this subject and it is an extremely tricky issue. Ageing as well as death are the two principal challenges to our belief that we are individuals. If we are always ageing and thus changing, how is it possible to define a constant notion of what makes up an individual? Do we have an essence? For many people this essence is classified as our soul and it is our souls which will pass into the next life. In many people's opinion the soul existed before we were born. In effect, in order to explain the conundrum of how we remain the same person whilst constantly changing, we divide ourselves into different parts and give one of those parts the role of being the constant me. However, even those who do not buy into the idea of a soul, believe that there are parts of their identity which can be regarded as permanent and others which are more changeable. Age is obviously changeable, and we all accept this, at least on a theoretical level. We all know that we are not the same at five as we are at 50. There are clearly a range of physical traits which we know change along with this. Hair colour, body hair, muscle tone, and height, to name but a few. Yet there are many other traits, especially ones based on people's characters, which we tend to regard as permanent ones. For example, generosity, kindness, stubbornness and avarice are all considered to be permanent, and the general belief is that we are born with these traits. Yet although my experience of life leads me to agree with this perspective, there are of course cases when people do change. An extreme example is where someone suffers from a brain injury such as a stroke and their character changes markedly. I have seen this in several people, where they seem to lose their inhibitions and say things that they would have never dared say before the injury. They cannot really be regarded as the same person as before the brain injury, yet from a legal and administrative perspective they definitely are (as long as they are still deemed capable of managing their own affairs). Extreme events demonstrate to us the changeable nature of our existence, because the rate of change is so much quicker than in normal life. Yet even in normal life, we all know that apparently unchangeable character traits do change even if very slightly. A tall person will lose some of their height as they go into later life, whilst a selfish person will only tend to get more selfish! Yes, the rate of change might be very slow, but that doesn't mean it is not taking place. So, in a sense, unless we believe in an unchangeable essence or soul, we accept that we are always changing, yet at the same time the social conventions which we base our lives on, implicitly include the idea of an unchangeable identity. This is of course completely paradoxical, yet at the same time inevitable, as if we didn't see the individual as at least to some extent a fixed entity, practical life on all levels would be impossible. What is even more ironic about this situation is that we use the principal measure of change in our lives, i.e. age, as a way of distinguishing people from each other. Age has over the last few decades become an absolutely defining factor in people's identities, along with gender.

Whenever someone is mentioned in the media, their age, sex, nationality (if relevant) and often racial origin are mentioned. In essence we are being given the basic parameters for imagining that individual. When we talk about social problems, they are always in relation to age, sex and social class. People's identities are merged into these classifications, as their commonalities are much stronger than their differences. This form of common identity not only helps others define particular social groups, but of course is an integral part of how people see themselves. Ageing is also one of the most striking examples of how a change in one aspect of our being affects how we view all the others. In this regard it is pretty obvious that a woman of 25 is unlikely to have the same view of what defines her as woman as a 75-year-old.

I have already spoken about language in terms of cementing the illusion that our world is real; however, it plays an equally important role in establishing our identity. Relations between people who share a similar language and culture (the two are intimately linked) are always going to be easier than between those of different cultures. There are always exceptions to this rule, but in general it holds true. For many peoples, language and its associated culture is the defining factor in their group identity. A good example is Germany, where long before there was a unified German state, the idea of Germanness was very important. In fact, the German peoples were quite spread out, with many groups living outside the traditional German territories, all over central and Eastern Europe. This idea of Germanness which was underpinned by a shared language and culture was a crucial element in the creation of a unified Germany in 1870. Its importance is illustrated by Bismarck, the German Chancellor at the time, who created a "Kulturkampf", or cultural campaign. He used

2. THE INDIVIDUAL

the idea of Germanness, or a common identity rooted in language and culture, to cement control over his new country. In the case of Germany, the common language and culture of a group of peoples, was the precursor to the creation of a state based on that common identity.

However, language is also used as a way of creating a national identity. An outstanding example is France, which never had a common language underpinning its identity. Until the First World War, France had a multitude of languages. Most of the south spoke the "langue d'oc" which is close to modern day Catalan; Celtic was spoken in Brittany; and the Basque language in the Basque region. It is only through the imposition of a national educational system, in which local languages were left out, that French gradually imposed itself as lingua franca of the entire French population. This process was not a random one but was specifically used in order to forge a national character and thus to strengthen the French Republic. It is much easier to persuade a population to follow you, if they feel part of the common culture that is your country. This process of using language to create a sense of nationality continues today. In the United States, which is very multi-cultural and multi-racial, the use of the English language to create a common culture is extremely important. To be a real American, it is absolutely essential for English to be your native tongue. First generation immigrants who have English as a second language or perhaps no language at all, will mostly feel firstly part of the country they come from and secondly American. However, their children, who will use English as their main language, are far more likely to feel completely American. In the UK, in order to become a citizen, it is now necessary to pass an English test. It is felt that it is simply not possible to bestow citizenship on someone who does not share the use of the national language.

There are also aspects of people's identity which are distinct from language or nationality. The most obvious of these is religion. Although both Christianity and Islam (the most populous religions by numbers) have specific geographical roots and have believers concentrated in some countries more than others, your nationality or culture of origin does not in any way stop you being accepted into the fold. This is also true of Jews who have lived spread out in many countries, spoken different languages and had different traditions. Yet they are still very strongly attached to their Jewish identity and for many Jews the most important aspect of their identity is their Jewishness. The idea that one of their children might marry a non-Jew could be a real problem for them. The same can be said for other religions, although in the case of Christianity or Islam, this is generally more easily solved if the person who is not of the same religion converts. These are all generalisations, of course, but the important point is that belief systems are an extremely important part of what make up our individual and common identity. For strong believers, religion is so important that it defines them in relation to non-believers. I have over the last

2. THE INDIVIDUAL

few years come across a number of fundamentalist Christians and I was somewhat surprised to discover that their religion was not simply something that gave them meaning and succour, but defined them in relation to non-believers, who could also be Christians yet did not have the same interpretation of the Bible as them. More than this, they viewed non-believers and especially followers of other religious faiths, e.g. Muslims, as a strong threat to them. The impression I got was that all non-believers were heading for hell and damnation, and only if you joined their particular brand of religion could you be saved. This type of behaviour seems to be quite typical although not in any way unanimous in religious belief. Your religion provides you with the certainty that only you and your fellow believers are right and that everyone else is lost. There are, of course, those who take this way of thinking to an extreme and are prepared to kill and maim for their beliefs. If this is so, then it is clear that religion plays an extremely important role in the creation of individual identity.

However, religion is not the only belief system which unites people in a common identity. Politics is another important example and can, as with religion, range from quite mild views to extremely radical and potentially dangerous ones. The worst massacres and genocides in the 20th century were all done in the name of political conviction. The most notable one of course is Nazism, which mixed nationalism with a political theory based on racial purity and state capitalism.

People were prepared to commit unspeakable crimes against their fellow human beings in the name of their political beliefs. For many of the propagators these beliefs enabled them to convince themselves that what they were doing was justified and right. They were able to commit atrocities against innocent men, women and children who (in the vast majority of cases) had not done anything to harm or offend them, simply for their beliefs. Whether their leaders were more cynical or not is completely beside the point, as the masses that carried out most of the crimes were able to bring themselves to do what they did at least partly because of belief. Or at the very least belief allowed them to justify their behaviour to themselves and their fellow believers. If the Nazi holocaust was the only example of its kind, we could probably put it down to a period of folly that would, thank god, never happen again. Unfortunately, even if we restrict our historical research to the 20th century, the examples are many and horrific. Whilst the Nazis were busy carrying out their holocaust against the Jews, Gypsies, communists and anyone else who didn't fit into their notion of a desirable human being, the Soviets under the leadership of Joseph Stalin, were busy dispatching millions of their own too. In fact, they had started somewhat earlier than the Germans, using tools such as mass starvation, forced migration and of course the good old-fashioned bullet in the back of the head. For the Soviets it was enough to be Ukrainian, a Cossack or simply a peasant farmer who was a little more successful than his neighbours in order to be worthy of extermination. The same pattern can be

2. THE INDIVIDUAL

discerned in the Rwandan holocaust, the Balkan mass murders and the many other examples of persecution and mass slaughter that have peppered our recent history. Of course, you could argue that it is power and political expediency rather than actual belief that drove this kind of behaviour; however, this is in a sense irrelevant, as in order to commit such crimes, the victims have to be defined as the other or a threat. They have to be differentiated and of course dehumanised in the eyes of the perpetrators, who frequently regard their victims as sub-human or of lesser value than them.

I think it is becoming clear that individuality or the sense we have of our own self is extremely fluid and is bound up with our sex, age, social background, political beliefs, and religion to name but a few parameters. But of course, in order to have an identity we first have to believe that we are distinct beings or individuals, able to move around in space and time.

Traditionally the individual is believed to be made up of their genetic inheritance, which is what distinguishes them at birth from their fellow human beings. Once they are born, the process of life will leave its imprint and with their genetic inheritance as a base, shape them into the individual they are. There are frequent arguments in both scientific and psychological circles as to the relative importance of these two influences. Many scientists tend to prefer the genetic approach as it is in a sense more solid than the experiential one. Many studies have been carried out using identical twins and comparing them at various stages of their lives. If as seems clear genes and individuality do exist, how can I claim that the individual is an illusion?

I am not foolish enough to discount the fact that there are differences between people! However, what is clear to me is that the notion we have of ourselves as individuals independent of our environment is a delusion. By this I don't mean that we are all mad, but rather that our individuality is an illusion, which appears at first glance to make perfect sense. But because it is based on the idea of a world which expands into the past and future, here and there it actually exists solely in our minds. It is like a mirage in the desert which when you get there and try to touch it simply disappears.

Although the reality is that we live in a constant now as an inseparable part of our immediate environment, it is the belief that we are separate, which creates our artificial world. As I have already discussed, in order for our notion of individuality to make sense, it has to be believed in by other human beings. Language is the primary mechanism for this shared view of the world. When someone does not have the same vision of the individual and society as the mainstream, they are unable to function and end up being labelled as mad. You have to buy into the same illusion as everyone else otherwise you are simply not going to fit in. Once we have been fully programmed, we look at our lives through the lens of our conditioning and often become completely incapable of seeing the world in a

2. THE INDIVIDUAL

more direct experiential way. When we are faced with experiences which don't seem to fit in, our tendency is to dismiss them as irrelevant.

If individuality is as I claim an illusion, why is it a problem and why is it at the root of our suffering? If it is not, then it really doesn't matter if our view of the world is a delusion or not! The essential conflict at the heart of the notion of individuality is between the fluidity and impermanence of life and the need to create a solid resilient self. It's quite difficult to see yourself as an individual if you accept that you are constantly changing. The other problem we face is that life is completely unpredictable and has no interest in our feelings, ideas or opinions. We can suffer all kinds of adversity at the drop of a hat, with no explanation or warning. For many of us this is a very big problem. In the old days, this used to be thought of as an act of God. People used to resort to sacrifices and prayers in order to try and ensure that they were well treated by fate. The belief was that life could not be random and that that there had to be a rational explanation for what went on. To them it was rational that the gods or god did this or that for a particular reason, whilst today we search for a rational scientific explanation. There is, however, no fundamental difference between these approaches, in that both are incapable of accepting that the future is completely unknowable and the past frequently inexplicable.

In order for us to believe that we are individuals we have to have a past and a future, we have to believe that our lives have a linear thread from our conception, right through until our theoretical deaths. In addition, we must see our lives as "independent" of our immediate environment, in as much as we are able to move around in the four dimensions and reflect on past and future events. In order for this to work we must also see other people and the rest of our universe in the same light. As I have already mentioned, the first problem that we have, is to face up to the fact that we can't control life. The artificial me is at the mercy of fate and even though we believe we have free will and can decide our future, we all know how this type of belief can be shattered. We are very vulnerable, and that vulnerability is a major problem for us. A classic example is when someone's loved one is struck down unexpectedly by an accident or illness, and they simply can't understand why it has happened to them. In our modern western society, the answer is often to try and find the cause and set up a pressure group to try and ensure that it never happens to anyone again. If they can ensure that their death ended up being useful to society, they find it a lot easier to cope with.

These are all coping mechanisms to ease the pain of unpredictability and impermanence, which dominates our lives. The real problem we face is not the immediate physical or emotional pain of injury, or loss, but rather the impact it has on the idea we have of ourselves in relation to those around us and the society we live in.

2. THE INDIVIDUAL

If a dog or cat is unable to have offspring this is not a problem for them because they have no expectation of it. However, for us humans it is a very big problem, not because we are unable to fulfil our genetic role, but because psychologically we are programmed to expect to be able to. Our perception of ourselves, which is intertwined with the opinion that society has of us, will be greatly affected, leading us to suffer psychologically. From a genetic perspective it is totally unimportant if the women who have babies through IVF were unable to do so. In fact, many people may say it will weaken the human race, because those who from the perspective of natural selection should not be reproducing are doing so. However, for those women, having children is extremely important, because it fulfils a psychological need that is a vital part of their feminine identity.

With the development of individuality, and recent technological advances, it appears that having children has changed from being a desire to a right. This change provides a perfect example of how one person's – or a couple's – attempt to bolster their own sense of identity may end up causing pain and suffering both for themselves and others. This is reflected in the different methods people employ to try and have children, some of which involve highly complex and extremely contentious moral issues. An excellent example is the issue of surrogate mothers, where a couple is prepared to pay another woman to carry their baby for them. In some countries such as France, this practice is banned, as it is viewed as an unacceptable commercialisation of women's bodies. This ends up creating very difficult moral and legal situations, as French women simply end up going abroad. The result is someone who is genetically the child of a French couple, but who from a legal perspective has no right to live in France. Not only does the child start off in the middle of a moral and legal battle, but furthermore later on in life he or she may well want to find out about the woman that bore him or her. The surrogate mother herself is unlikely to be able to live this kind of experience trouble-free. Are they always happy to let go of the child, and if they do what emotional scars will be left? There was a famous case in the United States known as "Baby M", where the surrogate mother refused to hand over the baby. In this case she was the actual biological mother and was in fact declared to be the legal mother of the child. Rather bizarrely, despite this ruling, the baby was handed over to the couple who had paid for her. There have been even more extraordinary cases where the genetic parents of a foetus, have tried to force the surrogate mother to have an abortion because of complications in the pregnancy. In these cases, whatever moral or legal position you may choose to take, it is clear that the desires of one person or group of persons, is going to have a significant impact on the lives of others. It can also, as illustrated by the above examples, lead to serious conflicts and emotional turmoil. Whilst it can be argued that the parties to the agreement, i.e. the parents and the surrogate mother, went into it with eyes wide open, the same cannot be said for the child. Such children may of course turn out to be happy, balanced individuals, but from my experience of adopted children, they are more than likely to want to find out about their origins. This is unlikely to be an easy process for them and the important point to make is that in these situations, the interests of the future children seem to be at the bottom of the list. This is starkly illustrated by the trend for much older women to have children using IVF. It is pretty obvious to me as a parent of young children that there is a good reason why nature has created a timeline for women's childbearing. Children are exhausting and very demanding, and on a very basic level you need lots of energy to be able to bring them up well. It's already hard enough doing this in your 20s, 30s and 40s, but is likely to become a real strain in your 50s and 60s. Furthermore, children don't only need us when they are small, but also as adults.

Another morally challenging example is the issue of "designer babies". I personally know of a case where a woman, because of her husband's cultural values, decided to have an IVF baby in order to ensure she had a boy. She was a fit fertile young woman who already had some girls, and could easily have conceived again naturally, but might of course have had another girl. The result was a pregnancy full of complications in which the baby was almost lost. Today there is even talk of being able to choose hair colour and other physical features.

I for one would have been extremely unhappy if my physical features had been chosen by my parents in order to satisfy their desires for the perfect child. Children are not objects to be ordered and designed to their parents' specifications, but autonomous beings, with their own feelings and (highly complex) identity. I am sure that with the developments now taking place in genetics, designer children will become a reality. Ever since man began to view himself as an individual, his desires have had an impact on those around him, but what modern fertility techniques have done, is to allow man to take his desires one step further. In a sense the same can be said for all of our technological developments. The pain and suffering that we endure due to the unpredictability of life is actually worsened a thousand times by the attempts we make to control our environment and the greater our ability to control it, the worse this situation becomes.

In many cases the impact we have on others is an unintended by-product of our actions and desires; however, humans also seem to have an ability, seemingly unfound in nature to deliberately inflict pain on others. If all we had to put up with in terms of suffering was the fact that nature threw some horrible things at us from time to time, life would in general be pretty good. Nature, it is true, is completely indifferent to our fate; however, one thing it is not is cruel. This particular characteristic is the special reserve of humankind! It is said that cruelty exists in other species. Apparently, cats like to play with their victims before they kill them and there are some other animals which display similar behaviour. However, it is pretty clear that this

2. THE INDIVIDUAL

kind of behaviour, even if it can be described as cruel (we may simply be applying human concepts to animal behaviour) pales in comparison to the human version. I have never heard of a cat locking up another cat for years on end and torturing it whenever the fancy takes it. It wasn't the cat who invented the rack, crucifixion, burning at the stake, the cutting off of limbs and all the other hideous forms of physical torture that humans have developed. Nor does the cat psychologically bully, belittle, ostracise or humiliate in the way us humans like to do whenever we need to boost our own sense of self-importance. It is clear that we have taken the infliction of all kinds of pain on other humans – and let's not forget, the animals – to an art form. In fact, we are so skilled at it, that it is said we are able to injure people without even noticing it!

I think it is becoming clear, that it is not simply our incapacity to accept the randomness of life but rather our reaction to this unpredictability that leads us to create suffering a thousand times worse for ourselves and others. The basic mechanism which underlies this process is our desire to bolster our own sense of self in the face of the fluid and changing world we inhabit. The more insecure we feel, the greater the degree of compensation required.

As I keep on repeating, it is the awareness we have of ourselves, which makes our lives so much more difficult than for animals. By being aware of ourselves we have desires, fears, hopes and thoughts, which go way beyond our immediate environment and place us in relation to things that don't exist, i.e. ideas. For an animal the immediate environment is the most important thing, whilst for us it has become at times almost irrelevant. We create our world, in the way I have already described, and we live in relation to it. A good example would be our career desires. From a young age we are told to think about the future and our entire educational system is based on this. At my 12-year-old son's school, it was made clear recently that if us parents wanted a bright future for him, we needed to get involved in his education. How many times do parents tell their children "don't you care about your future?" or at least that is what the classical American teenage film depicts. This approach is based on the fear that our child will not succeed in society and will therefore have no value as an individuals. We need our child to tick the boxes required by society in order for us to feel good about ourselves as parents. To validate our own notion of individuality our children must perform well as social beings, allowing us to bask in the reflected glow of their success. By making our children base their actions on an idea of the future, we are ever more firmly anchoring them in our socialised but illusory concept of existence.

Life, however, as I have already mentioned, is totally unpredictable, both in terms of human and natural activity. As we always interpret everything that happens in terms of how it affects us, we live in a constant state of hope and fear with events causing us to swing between these extremes. Of course, some

2. THE INDIVIDUAL

people are naturally much more balanced and are less affected by the (6) "slings and arrows of outrageous fortune" as William Shakespeare puts it. However, the essential instability and unpredictability of life makes us incredibly insecure. Our answer is to find ways of bolstering ourselves up, but unfortunately this process is not without its cost. Childhood behaviour provides a classic example, as the ego manifests itself without the normal social constraints that adults have learnt to live with. A child is desperately trying to establish their identity, and this will involve a sense of self-importance. This type of behaviour is almost standard among siblings. One child will deliberately steal something off another or exclude them from a game with the intention of establishing their superiority. It is a manifestation of the pecking order which gives a person a sense of who they are. Of course, this type of thing happens with animals; however, equilibrium is usually quickly established. With humans, because the establishment of such a pecking order has gone beyond instinct and into the realm of psychology the stakes are much higher. Because we have a sense of self awareness, which is relative to the knowledge that other beings exist, we have a very strong temptation to confirm our own existence through having power over others. It is because those others recognise our power and importance that we feel better about ourselves. Because the rest of a class clearly respects and admires me, my existence is undeniable and of importance. It doesn't matter that I change all the time or that I will die, because my own sense of self is confirmed by the reaction of others. It is the most powerful type of drug around and like all drugs it only works for short periods. However much adulation, love or fear you may receive from others, the effect is always short lived as doubt will always creep back. You will always need to go back for more. It is an endless and pointless search for the drug of self-confirmation.

There are, of course, those who are more or less indifferent to the problem of impermanence and take life as it comes. They are not free of suffering but find hardship much easier to cope with. On the other hand, there are those for whom life is a constant battle to prove their importance and for these people failure or loss can be devastating. These differences do not, however, change the fundamental problem but are merely different ways of coping with it. The important point to note is that the bigger the problem it is for someone, the more likely they are to try and find an extreme solution. This is likely to be painful for both them and the people they are involved with. Racism is a case in point. Its premise is that you and the other human beings whom you regard as being similar to you are superior to another group. The very fact that you believe this is a huge boost to your ego which will feel much more secure as a result. The fact that you are of more value than another person, means that you must exist as an independent entity. Furthermore, not only do you exist but your existence is worth more than other people's, meaning that your existence is particularly important!

2. THE INDIVIDUAL

Life for us humans is basically a constant and fruitless struggle for the confirmation of our existence. We are stuck in a giant vicious circle, where we suffer because of our own insecurity and then take action to make ourselves feel better. The type of action will depend on the type of person we are but will always accentuate the problem in the long term for ourselves and most probably for others. In the modern world one of the principal symptoms of this process is our obsessive consumption and its main manifestation: money.

3. MONEY

Our society has been, and is, dominated by an incredibly strong desire to earn, spend and of course accumulate money. Yes, we might often hear that "money is at the root of all evil"; however, this does not stop it from dominating our world. Even people living in relatively poor societies strive to acquire goods that are not strictly necessary for survival. Trekking through the Atlas Mountains in Morocco recently, I was surprised to see a proliferation of satellite dishes and solar panels. Other than that, the villages did not seem to have changed much for hundreds of years. The houses were made of mud and there was no electricity or running water. For these simple mountain people, acquiring such examples of 21st century living was obviously considered very important, yet for many, it must have been a real struggle to afford.

This desire to acquire the trappings of wealth, whether it is a satellite dish for a Moroccan peasant farmer or a super yacht for a Russian oligarch, is by far the most

3. MONEY

dominant of the forces which shape our world today. We are constantly bombarded by images of what money can bring us, whether this is a holiday in the Caribbean, a new smartphone, or the latest clothing fashion. It is impossible to escape and permeates every aspect of our existence. The underlying message behind all these images is that by being able buy any of these goods and services you will improve your life in some way or other. This is the message behind almost all advertising, whether it is for cars, telephones or deodorant. By owning and using their product, your existence will be better. You will feel better because you own this desirable and enjoyable car, you will smell better because of this long lasting and fragrant deodorant, or you will look younger and therefore have better self-esteem because you are using "X" face cream. Even adverts, whose only message is about saving you money, are part of the same paradigm. By saving you money you will have more money to spend on other things, which means that you will be able to make yourself feel even better. Simply put, the more money you have the better you will feel, because you will be able to buy all these fantastic products which will dramatically improve your lives. This is the message behind almost all consumer advertising, and we can see and hear it all around us most of the time. Every time you turn on your TV, computer or radio, travel by car, train or plane, or simply walk along a city street, you are bombarded by advertising. When you begin to actually analyse it, it is amazing that we can cope with it. We are in effect being bombarded with incessant images telling us that our lives are inadequate because we don't have this product or another, or haven't seen such a film or visited such a place. Furthermore, what is being sold is not even the product but the image that goes with it. So, for example, car adverts don't simply concentrate on the practical and driving features of the car but rather the self-image that we feel owning such a car will bring. This is exactly the same phenomenon behind the explosion of designer labels in recent years. If people can be persuaded that merely to own something with a particular label will enhance their sense of self-worth, then that label is going to find selling extremely easy. They are probably going to be able to make huge profits because what they are selling is the image of the label rather than simply a product. They can then sell something which may only be of marginally better quality than its non-label competitors, but has a huge price premium. This is why people are even willing to steal designer clothes off people's backs, as happened in the 2011 London riots.

Of course, image-based advertising has been with us for a long time, and was an important part of cigarette advertising until it was banned in the West. I remember even now some of the classic cigarette adverts, including the Marlboro ad which featured the classic American cowboy the "Marlboro Man" smoking his Marlboro cigarette. The image that was being portrayed was that smoking was cool, and that was certainly the view I had of it when I was a teenager. You didn't just smoke because you liked the taste and effect, but because you felt cool doing so and this perception was in large part created by the tobacco companies. This process dominates the lives of most people living in developed consumer economies, and is of course never ending. We will only be fleetingly satisfied by any of these purchases as all consumer companies and their advertising agencies well know. Of course, they not only know this but actively encourage the process, as it would be totally against their interests for it to stop. In fact, companies constantly strive to render yesterday's product obsolete, either by creating a new far more desirable one, or otherwise by building obsolescence into their products. So, in the case of cutting-edge products such as mobile phones, it is simply a question of bringing out the new model or even better a completely new type of device, and through marketing and advertising make everyone want to buy them. But with rather simpler and more utilitarian products such as toasters or kettles, they simply make products which fall apart after a few years. What is in fact happening is a process in which our natural sense of insecurity is being manipulated in order to persuade us to spend the money which most of us will have worked to acquire. The process is a circular one as the only reason that these companies are behaving in this way is so that they themselves can earn money in order to fill the pockets of the management and shareholders. They will then use the money that they have earned to in turn consume other goods and services. In general, their aim is to earn as much money as possible, even if they will have difficulty spending even a fraction of it. It seems that there is almost no level of wealth which satisfies people and once people start making a lot of money, they generally do not stop. Why do people who already have hundreds of millions of dollars or even billions continue to make more? It seems to be an insatiable process that provides them with no benefits at all, bar the satisfaction of having been able to do it and perhaps being more successful than others. It certainly cannot be a sign that we are happy with the way we are and that we feel secure and comfortable in our role as individuals, otherwise we would not constantly feel that there is something lacking in our lives.

What is even stranger about this phenomenon is that in the case of many big companies, there are no easily identifiable owners. They are often large pension funds, who effectively belong to the general working population. What you have is your money which you are saving up to pay for your retirement, seeking to make more money out of you. On the surface it seems that money almost has a mind of its own! In fact, it seems that apart from those at the very bottom of the pile, i.e. the indentured child labourers in developing countries, almost everyone feels that they benefit from the system. We are all trapped in a belief system, whereby we feel that earning money and then spending it to consume various goods and services, the vast majority of which are not necessary for survival, enhances our lives. Or at least we believe this to be the case at the time, even if sub-consciously, we might have a nagging sense that it is not really the answer to our problems. Nevertheless, this does not stop people ruining their health, their lives and the health and lives of others in the pursuit of material enrichment.

Yet money's influence does not simply involve a desire to acquire the trappings of wealth. Its impact is much more pervasive than that, and affects every aspect of our existence. One of the most obvious examples is the way we treat each other as individuals. I have already discussed in my chapter on the individual, how the way we view ourselves and others is highly fluid and complex. It is affected among other factors by age, ethnicity, class, nationality, gender, religion and political affiliation. Yet for many people it is money that is the real yardstick by which they judge how well they have succeeded in life and also how they view and treat other people.

This is not to deny the importance of belief systems, friendships or family ties, but rather to point out that even in these spheres money has an influence. We all know the impact of money on family behaviour. Even in the best-balanced family, the way parents distribute money, by for example helping one child out more than another, can easily upset the other siblings. In more imbalanced families, money can have totally disastrous impacts. In my little village in France I know of a few families where siblings are at war over their inheritance. They may live two doors down from each other but will not exchange a word. In society in general there are countless examples of this type of thing and in extreme cases people will even resort to murder to achieve their aims.

Even in spheres such as religion, money quickly rears its ugly head. One of the principal reasons for the reformation was the perception by many people that religion was simply a way of controlling and taxing them. It is well known that priests sold certificates guaranteeing that you would go to heaven. For the longest time the choice of Pope and Cardinals was based on family and rank, and was for many a way of enriching themselves further. The monasteries of medieval and early renaissance Europe were incredibly rich and powerful. Nor can this association between religion and wealth be regarded as something that belongs to the past. The relatively recent machinations of the Vatican bank, with its supposed links to the mafia, suggest that money still has a powerful hold over the way people in the Church behave. This is also illustrated by many of the evangelical churches that exist, particularly in the USA, who can be pretty brazen about their appeals for money.

Furthermore, money or the desire for it seems to lead us to behave in ways which are blatantly counter to our own well-being. Why is it that so many of us do jobs merely for money? The obvious answer is because we need it to survive, but as I have just pointed out this is actually rarely the case. If survival was all we cared about, most people could get by with a lot less and would not work themselves to the bone in order to

3. MONEY

acquire material goods. You cannot say that the Berber villagers of Morocco whom I came across during my holiday needed satellite dishes and TVs, yet they were prepared to work extremely hard in order to be able to afford them. Yet even though they desire the material goods which money brings them, for many people work can be a source of misery. Think of the number of people who do jobs which others wouldn't dream of doing because it is the only way they can earn a crust. The cleaners, dustmen, abattoir workers and washer-uppers and other low paid workers probably don't do their jobs out of love. Even many of the people in white collar jobs are only doing their jobs to get by, and this is starkly illustrated by the obsession we have with retirement. People who do their jobs because they love them, almost never want to retire. How many painters, writers, musicians, and even politicians stop working at retirement age?

Because almost everyone buys into this way of thinking, most social relations are based on this paradigm. For example, the vast majority of our social interactions are for economic reasons. Whether it is the baker, the dentist, the bus conductor, the taxi driver, the shop assistant or the bank teller, if you had no money you would be far less likely to get a friendly reception. In fact, although it is by no means the only factor, our wealth is extremely important in how people treat us. We all know that the rich get better treatment than the poor. Anyone who has had the dubious privilege of travelling on a budget airline will know that those who can afford first class will not have the same experience at all.

Furthermore, our work which for most people is about making or earning money, plays an absolutely essential role in defining who we are. Our job will normally define how much money we earn, which then has an impact on the entire way we live. What type of house we can afford, where that house is, what clothes we wear, what car we drive, the type of schools we send our children to, and so on and so forth. In general, someone who has a high paying job will probably mix with other people from the same social group and will probably choose his or her life partner from that group. Of course, a lot of this may have been influenced by that person's own background, but their work life will be a manifestation of their own identity.

Even areas of activity such as healthcare, which one would imagine had nothing to do with money, are strongly influenced by it. I worked for a while in a doctor's practice and was very surprised to see the number of things that had been provided by the drug companies. Pens, mugs and stationery all seemed to have the logos of various pharmaceutical companies on them. On a regular basis a rep would turn up and provide lunch for the whole practice. Until then I had naively believed that doctors chose the medicines, that they prescribed on the basis of matching the best remedy to the patient's condition and not on which rep had provided the best lunch! Furthermore, pharmaceutical companies do not

3. MONEY

only restrict themselves to buttering up doctors and practice managers, but will also lobby governments directly to buy their drugs. They do this directly and also through their use of media campaigns. An example might be a new cancer drug that is deemed to be too expensive for a country's healthcare system to afford. It is not too difficult to create a press storm by finding those that are unable to get the supposedly "miracle treatment". Another way that sales of medicines are increased is by direct advertising to the public. It is amazing the number of medicines that are advertised often with some quite eye-popping messages. One that particularly shocked me was an advert I saw in London for an anti-flu medication which told people that it would enable them to keep going to work with the flu. The main benefit was that being able to stay at work would stop colleagues from getting ahead of them in their job. Firstly, it seems incredible from a public health perspective that this type of advert is allowed. If you are ill, especially with a virus, the last thing that you want to be doing is going to work and giving it to everyone. Secondly, it is unlikely to be good for that person's health to be working when they are ill. Quite honestly, it has always struck me as extraordinary that this type of advertising is legal. As I have already said, my naïve belief was always that you took medicines because you needed them, because the doctor believed them to be the best way to get you back to health and not for the sole reason of making huge profits for big pharma.

So not only is most human activity driven by the desire to accumulate money, but the impact of this process is far from beneficial. It is arguable that it is the cause of most wars, environmental damage, poverty and all kinds of trafficking and trading which result in pain and suffering. To me it has always seemed odd, that we want to conserve our environment, protect indigenous peoples, and bring help to those suffering from hunger and extreme poverty, yet never ask ourselves why they are in this situation. We seem simply to accept that it is the case and concentrate our efforts on trying to put a plaster on it. Many people will even passionately deny that the immediate cause is the drive for profit and will argue that liberal capitalism is generally beneficial to societies. Yes, there may be some unwanted side-effects, but dealing with these is just a question of good management. Wealth creation helps to lift people out of poverty and enables their society to move towards a free and democratic society in which individuals and their rights are valued and respected. In a sense the opinions of particular individuals about this, is more or less irrelevant as the process seems to be unstoppable. Movements such as communism which tried to create societies, in which the drive for profit was eliminated, have manifestly failed and quickly turned into Oligarchies based on a type of state capitalism. This was the case with the Soviet Union, China, and all the other so-called "communist countries".

Surely the central point is not whether liberal capitalism is the best type of society but rather why do we have such a need to accumulate material goods at all? The answer to this must lie in the relationship between money and individuality, which have developed alongside each other since money began many thousands of years ago. For a long time now the ownership of property has been one of the principal defining features of being an individual, with money as its most obvious manifestation. Ownership enables our illusory world to manifest itself in a material form, and in doing so it provides concrete evidence of our existence and our importance. Social class which accompanies it, further reinforces this notion as it enables us to believe that we are better than other people. By being richer and more important, my existence is confirmed as having value, because another person's life clearly has less importance than my own. This type of thinking has obviously spread into family life and into other forms of group identity. Philosophically speaking, by having money and ownership we are taking control of our environment and of our lives. We have gone so far away from behaving as though we are a part of our environment that we now believe that it all belongs to us. In doing so we have gradually come to believe that our illusory world is the real world and that our individuality is as real as the ground we stand on. I believe that it is almost inevitable that once we start believing that we have lives independent of our immediate environment, and are able to move around in an artificial world of time and space which exists 100% in our heads, we will seek to construct "individuality" using artifice. Ownership is in a sense the ultimate artifice, because in order to own you have to exist, and furthermore you can show other people what you own. Why else would we take such pleasure in driving around in expensive cars, wearing designer clothes, living in houses which all our acquaintances and friends can see? Of course, you have those that prefer to be discreet, but even if they don't spend their time showing their wealth off to everyone else, they can comfort themselves with the knowledge of what they own. What is doubly extraordinary about this situation, is that not only are almost all societies equally guilty of this behaviour, but almost no one even begins to question it. Perhaps it is because the moment we begin to question the basis of materialism and money, we question our individuality, something we simply cannot afford to do.

Yet money has not always been with us and it is believed that in the free giving societies which existed before it, goods and services were given without any expected reward or exchange. It is doubtful in these situations that people thought of those goods as being theirs in the way we do today. As over time money and an economy based on the exchange of goods and services has slowly developed, our sense of individuality and ownership has progressed alongside. As I have already discussed, the world in which more primitive societies lived was a much more local and immediate one. They did not have the tools that we have today, to create the vast imaginary reality which we inhabit. They had to wait for the development of calendars, clocks, maps, sextants and more recently all the modern systems

3. MONEY

we have for mapping and measuring our world. The slow development of money into the vastly complex financial universe which now exists, accompanied the gradual development of human society from a very basic agrarian one to the complex one we now inhabit. This massively accelerated with the development of capitalism, which slowly replaced feudalism as the dominant social and economic system. Under feudalism social relations were dominated by land ownership, and feudal relationships between lords and vassals. Those further down the social ladder gave a portion of what they produced to their immediate superior who in turn gave a portion to their lord. The King, who was at the top of the pyramid, dominated everything and at least in theory handed out and took away all social and economic power. However, today social relations are dominated by money and it is the ability to make money or at least keep what you have, which underpins your position in society. Interestingly enough, one of the principal changes that accompanied the move from a feudal to a capitalist system, was the increasing importance of individuals and their rights. The French revolution, which was one of the seminal events in the change from a feudal to a modern democratic world, included a declaration that is one of the principal foundations of the modern world. This is the (7) "Declaration of the rights of man" of 1789. Its first clause which states "Men are born and remain free and equal in rights" makes it absolutely clear that an individual is a separate entity with innate rights. A later clause goes on to say that "Since property is an inviolable and sacred right, no one shall be deprived thereof except where public necessity, legally determined, shall clearly demand it..." There is no doubt here, that the ownership of property is considered an integral part of what makes up an individual. This is the culmination of a long slow process in which the idea of individuality evolved from a very limited sphere, to today's rights-based world. Property has clearly been around for a very long time, at least as long as money, and we know that money has played an important role in human society for thousands of years. Yet although individual ownership existed, it was not considered an inseparable and inviolable part of what it meant to be a human being. Nor did human rights exist as they do today. Of course, there were moral codes but there is a fundamental difference between these and today's rights-based culture. In most pre-enlightenment religions, which were in a sense the cradle of these moral beliefs, man was considered to be God's creature and to a large extent the way his life unfolded was dependent on God's will. Man was not viewed as completely independent and able to exist in a separate bubble. During the Renaissance with the development of a humanist or human-centred approach this began to change as humans came to be viewed as in charge of their destiny. Gradually humans started seeing themselves as being completely separate from their environment, both psychologically and practically. One of the main technological changes which accompanied this process was the development of time. Most of us are probably unable to imagine a world in which time, as we know it, simply didn't exist.

3. MONEY

Yet for most rural people in medieval Europe, life revolved around the seasons and precise time keeping played no role at all. Furthermore, the physical world which people inhabited was much smaller, with many people never leaving their locality and often having little or no idea what existed more than a few miles away, let alone in other countries or continents. Most of the world was unexplored and even the "known" parts of the world were generally unmapped, at least in any meaningful sense. This began to change as an abstract concept of time began to be introduced into society. Starting in the Italian city states during the 14th century with the construction of clock towers, its impact would be revolutionary. Modern time allowed people to expand their world and develop the concept of individuality outside of the immediate physical environment in which they lived. This was absolutely essential to the development of commerce as if you wish to trade you need to be able to plan and organise things into the future. Contracts need to be dated and have fixed periods of time for which they are applicable. If you are going to lend someone some money, the interest rate and the term of repayment needs specific periods to function. Without these parameters, these types of commercial contracts would make no sense at all. It is no coincidence that the modern financial system began in the Italian city state. Of course, commerce including financial transactions had existed for a long time and had been part of the Roman and Greek worlds. However, the invention of sophisticated time keeping mechanisms allowed the development of a much more complex and wide-ranging commercial and financial systems. At the same time, the change from the medieval to a humanist perception of the world, involved a seismic shift in which man began to take control of his fate. In the medieval world, events were very much put down to being God's will, and man did not make much of an effort to understand how things worked or what causes lay behind events. However, with humanism this all began to change, as man began to seek to understand how his world worked and of course how to control it. This was a gradual process which has subsequently affected every single area of our life.

Through a combination of economic, social and technological changes our world has been totally transformed. We went from an agrarian-based social and economic system governed by rigid social structures, where religion dominated and access to knowledge was highly restricted to today's hugely complex information-based world. Prior to the invention of printing in 1440, very few people could read and write with most literate people belonging to the Church. Books were all handwritten and as a result very few copies were made with the books being closely guarded. The information available to the average person was extremely limited and as a result their awareness of what went on outside their immediate world, negligible. Contrast this with today's information-rich world, where at the touch of a button it is possible to find facts, opinions and all kinds of media products on anything and everything. The net result of this change is a vast expansion in the extent

3. MONEY

of our shared illusory world. In a medieval village, it is most unlikely that anyone could read – there were no clocks, no electricity, and no organised postal system. Their world was tiny compared to that of today and even though they had a sense of yesterday and tomorrow, here and there its significance was much more limited. Communities and families were much more important and the ability to live in isolation as many people do now was simply not feasible. People had to live by the seasons in terms of their working day, the food they could eat, and their ability to travel. Money played an extremely small role in their lives, with most people living a subsistence lifestyle, and paying their taxes with the food they grew. Relations with other people were determined mostly by social rank, and social and family ties. Yes, the individual existed, but the scope of their action was far smaller and so was the importance of money.

Since time immemorial humans have been at the mercy of natural forces; however, with the advent of the modern world we have increased our vulnerability even further. If your world is very small, and you cannot imagine much into the future or far away from where you are, the potential causes of problems are more limited. Things which are outside your world are simply not going to affect you or even if they do you are not aware of the impact until it hits you. Today, because we think far into the future, and most of our world exists way beyond our immediate environment, we are at the mercy of forces which simply didn't exist before. A good example is the economic cycles which have accompanied capitalism since it began 800 or 900 years ago. As we have seen, these are intimately linked with the financial system, and when a crash happens, we are almost all affected in a multitude of ways. Firstly because of our information-rich world we are aware that the crash has happened and that our lifestyles are likely to be affected, we are afraid. Even if it turns out that we are not actually affected that badly by what happens, we have still suffered because of the worry that we might. Of course, if our lives are impacted, we are going to suffer a good deal more as we might lose our job, and even our house, which will in turn affect our relationships. Our sense of self is likely to be severely threatened by this and many people will be badly affected both psychologically and physically. An extreme example of this was stockbrokers jumping out of windows during the Wall Street crash! The more developed we have become, the greater our individuality and the more our world is dependent on extraneous factors, with money being the primary example. Paradoxically we have created an artificial bubble which in one way protects us from the natural world, but actually creates ever more outside forces which can threaten us. Our houses protect us from the vagaries of weather and the seasons, our water is cleaned before we use it, and our waste is treated. We wear clothes and travel around in hermetically sealed boxes. Yet despite this plethora of protective features, we are actually incredibly vulnerable. This was starkly illustrated to me by my travels to India and Nepal when I was in my 20s. Firstly we had to get vaccinated, then we had to take pills against malaria and of course we had to stick to drinking mineral water. Despite this I managed to get dysentery and giardia and returned home almost 20kg lighter; looking as though I had just emerged from a famine. In fact, whenever I make the mistake of visiting countries with less developed public health systems than my own, I end up getting a life-threatening disease. I am the perfect example of the modern individual who is totally dependent on the artificial bubble of the modern world in order to survive. When I step out of it, my health and even my life is quickly placed at risk.

Nowhere is this more evident than in the most important industry of all: agriculture. Although I am no scientist and have almost no knowledge of horticulture, I have noticed that the principal challenge of agriculture seems to be coping with pests and diseases of various types. Where I live, we have a lot of organic farmers, and I know that a huge part of their work is manually weeding their fields. In an environment where there has never been any agriculture and people hunt and gather, these problems simply don't exist. Humans function as part of the ecosystem and, bar adverse natural events, everything remains in balance. Of course, everything is in a constant state of change, and species come and go, but on a day-to-day basis you do not have to fight with nature to produce your food. Modern agriculture has, of course, developed pest and disease controlling chemicals which may be effective but almost inevitably pollute the environment and adversely affect our health.

In fact, Jared Diamond (8) argues that the change from a hunter gatherer lifestyle to one based on agriculture has been an unmitigated disaster for the human race. He starts by saying that archaeology has begun to demolish one of the most fundamental assumptions about human civilisation; namely that human history has been a long tale of progress. He goes on to say that the adoption of agriculture was not a great leap forward towards a better life but rather the greatest mistake ever made by the human race. On the face of it this argument seems absurd. Today we don't have to worry about where our next meal will come from; we live in better conditions, are healthier and live longer than ever before. We are incredibly advanced technologically and have been far more productive artistically than during any other period. However, he counters this by saying that whilst the above might be true for the wealthiest part of the global population, especially in recent times, it was definitely not the case for those who originally adopted agriculture or even for many of the people alive today. If you compare the lives of some of the few remaining hunter gatherer groups with the rest of us, at first it would seem obvious that their lives are harder. However, these groups have more leisure time, sleep a lot and work much less hard than their farming neighbours. The Hazda nomads of Tanzania devote only 14 hours or less a week gathering food, far less than the traditional farmer. Furthermore, the diet of these hunter gatherers is much richer in protein and the nutrients found in wild plants than the farmers who concentrate on growing high carbohydrate crops like maize or potatoes. Diamond goes on to state that "In one study, the Bushmen's average daily food intake (during a month when food was plentiful) was 2,140 calories and 93 grams of protein, considerably greater than the recommended daily allowance for people of their size. It's almost inconceivable that Bushmen (hunter gatherers from Southern Africa), who eat 75 or so wild plants, could die of starvation the way hundreds of thousands of Irish farmers and their families did during the potato famine of the 1840s. The lives of the world's last remaining hunter gatherers are not dominated by the uncomfortable struggle for survival we imagine."

However, their lives cannot realistically represent life on earth before the development of agriculture. Fortunately, the development of paleopathology or the study of signs of disease in ancient peoples has enabled us to analyse very precisely what these people ate and how healthy they were. These findings are based on skeletons, but enable us to deduct a surprising amount of information. These include the owner's sex, weight and approximate age. It is also possible to measure growth rates, signs of malnutrition and determine whether the person had suffered or was suffering from certain diseases. One extremely interesting finding related to the difference in height between hunter gatherers and early farmers. Around the end of the last ice age, the average height of hunter gatherers based on skeletons found in Greece and Turkey was 5ft 9" for men and 5ft 5" for women. With the adoption of agriculture average height fell dramatically until by 300BC average height for men had fallen to 5ft 3" and to 5ft for women. Even modern-day Turks and Greeks have not regained the height of their ancestors!

Other studies show that the change from a hunter gatherer lifestyle to farming had a negative effect on longevity and health. Average life expectancy dropped from 26 years to 19 years, and there was a three-fold increase in infectious diseases and a significant increase in degenerative diseases of the spine, most likely the result of hard physical labour. Unsurprisingly, a number of specialists believe that people switched to farming from hunter gathering by necessity rather than choice!

Diamond himself cites three principal reasons why agriculture was bad for people's health. Firstly, the diet of a hunter gatherer was much more varied and nutritious, whilst early farmers got most of their food from one or several starch-based crops. Secondly, farming peoples are at much greater risk of starvation as one crop can easily fail; and thirdly, because agriculture encouraged people to live in more crowded societies, which traded with other crowded societies, parasites and infectious diseases spread much more easily. Epidemics can't take hold in populations made up of small bands of people constantly on the move with diseases such as measles and the bubonic plague requiring cities to be able to spread and thrive.

3. MONEY

The development of farming was also one of the key steps in the creation of our modern money-based world. Hunter gatherers have almost no stored food and consequently no real notion of stored wealth. They generally get the food they need on a day-to-day basis. In their world there are no social classes and no concept of one group of people becoming richer than the others. Money simply makes no sense in the hunter gatherer world and it took the establishment of a system where food could be stored for the future, to enable the development of money and other forms of wealth. This is a psychological as much as an economic step, as in order to store food for the future you need to have an idea of the future. Farming requires you to work now with a notion of how it will benefit you at some future date. Your world needs to extend way beyond your immediate world, to the time and space where you will be able to harvest your crops. And in this way the scope of our illusory reality began to accelerate with very significant practical and social consequences. As Jared Diamond has pointed out, whilst farming has allowed us to live in far greater numbers, the consequences of such a shift are far from being 100% positive.

Although Mr Diamond calls the shift from hunter gathering to farming "the worst mistake in the history of the human race", it is pretty clear that it was not really choice but rather necessity which made us take this path. Because of our ability to plan and organise ourselves, we gradually became too successful for our world, and became unable to continue living off the fat of the land. Farming was the only solution which would enable us to continue expanding in terms of population and geographical reach. Once farming became established, it was also inevitable that property and social class would emerge as well as all the other distinguishing features of our modern world. As such, money is not an independent evil which can somehow be got rid of to enable a utopia to emerge as many political theories would have us believe, but rather an inevitable consequence of the development of individuality and the illusory reality upon which it depends for existence.

From what I am saying it may seem that I am harking back to the good old days and portraying progress as the cause of all our problems! However, to believe this would be naïve and it is clear that humans have been suffering for as long as we can remember. It is having a sense of individuality at all, however limited, that is the primary problem. Our egos are a little bit like the Genie, who once let out of the bottle has a life of his own. Once the individual exists, they will do everything in their power to try and shore up their existence. This is, of course, not something done by one person but rather collectively, with the result being a world in which individuality plays an ever-important role.

In short, although money is the apparent cause of most of our problems, it is itself merely an effect of or an attempt to compensate for the insecurity we all feel as a result of not existing in the way we believe we do. Individuals, as I have already mentioned, do not exist as

3. MONEY

fixed entities, but are fluid and changeable beings who struggle to maintain their identity. Material wealth is one of the principal ways that we seek to shore up and strengthen our identities in the face of all the challenges that are thrown at us. It does not, of course, exist on its own but is mixed up with the other mechanisms we use to strengthen our identities such as family, religion, nationality, race and gender to name but a few. If we take the example of the British Empire, nationalism, religion and notions of racial superiority were all used to justify what was essentially an economic project. The reason for colonialism was fundamentally financial and when having colonies became unviable economically, they were quickly abandoned. The same can be said for the US today, where ideas such as democracy and freedom are often used as justifications for the advancement of American economic interests. In some cases where America has backed brutal dictators, the justification has been the stopping of the spread of Communism, which threatens freedom and democracy on a global level. These types of examples can be found again and again in history, and merely illustrate the extraordinary human ability to make things fit into their reality.

Money does not exist separately from everything else that makes up our world, but is rather one of the easily identifiable facets of civilisation. It is a bit like trying to understand the functioning of the human body, by separating out different aspects of our physiology. It may make it easier to understand, but no body part or biological system can make sense on its own because everything is completely interlinked and part of everything else. We cannot, therefore, blame our suffering and our problems on money, but need to see it as an inevitable aspect of the human condition. As long as we persist in believing that we are somehow separate from the world around us, and in control of our environment, we will have wealth and exploitation. This may seem a very harsh way of seeing the world, but I am unable to imagine any other scenario. Once one is able to see the illusory nature of time and space, and therefore the individual, it becomes absolutely clear that all other problems flow from this. You can tinker with human society as much as you like, by making it richer, fairer and better organised. However, you will never alter the basic paradox at the heart of our existence, which has led to the creation of money and all the other ultimately pointless compensatory mechanisms we have vainly created to try to square the circle.

4. MORALITY

The concepts of good and evil have played a role in human society since time immemorial and continue to do so today. However, this does not stop them from being as artificial as all the other concepts which make up our world, completely dependent on our sense of individuality and the existence of a space-time framework.

Without a notion of good and evil as an underlying concept, which as I have just stated depends on us having an idea of our existence as separate beings, morality makes no sense at all. A moral sense requires both reflection and intention as well as an ability to assess both actions and thoughts against some kind of measuring rod. As such, it is not just a set of practical rules which become ingrained into us when we are young, but a conscious aspect of who we are as individuals. The development of morality as an abstract concept is like property and money, an inevitable part of the development of individuality. A person who is not an individual with no concept of time or space and thus unable to view themselves as being separate from their immediate environment cannot be considered to have any moral sense.

Furthermore, morality is completely dependent on people being viewed and seeing themselves as responsible for their actions. As humans we are conscious of what we have done, and what we intend to do in the future. We are then capable of assessing these actions in the light of our morality. As a rule, we are taught to look before we leap, which means that we need to weigh up our actions in the light of the effect they may have on ourselves and of course on others. This process requires us to accept that we are responsible for our actions both in the short and long term. In turn, this sense of responsibility depends upon us having a defined sense of self, which of course has a past and a future. In reality, it's a chicken and egg situation as one cannot really exist without the other. Clearly you cannot have a sense of moral responsibility without a sense of individuality, but at the same time, the moment you create a sense of self which is considered in some way permanent you will automatically think about the impact of what you have done. Furthermore, as I have already described, individuality is based on a world artificially divided up by time and space. Our actions are time-based and are intended to have an effect which will be observable in the future. Of course, this is also the case to some extent in the animal world. For example, when a predator stalks his prey, it is clearly

4. MORALITY

with a future-based intention of eating it. However, although it is not possible to say for certain without being an animal oneself, I imagine that this behaviour is instinctive and does not involve an internal moral debate beforehand! Whilst humans are also capable of behaving instinctively, any action whose effect is intended to be in a place distant both spatially and time-wise from our immediate environment requires us to reflect on it.

This is something which is implicitly accepted in legal systems, so for example if someone is thought to have diminished responsibility they are not considered to be responsible for what they have done. All moral judgements, whether in the private or public sphere, or even if someone judges themselves, only make sense if the actions which are being judged belong to that person. So just as with property, ownership even if understood in a different way is an essential part of morality's makeup. This in turn depends on having a concept of a person who existed in the past and will continue to exist in the future.

Because our lives as individuals have gone way beyond instinct and simple learnt behaviour, we have developed much more complex behavioural rules than animals. Of course, the more intelligent the animal the more complex its world may be and it is clear that the world of a chimpanzee is much more complicated than that of a goldfish! However, as far as I am aware, no animal has yet reached a point where they can separate themselves sufficiently from their environment so as to believe that they are independent beings. Of course, it is not possible to fully understand and judge the behaviour of other animals, and it is possible that some of them may be a good deal more advanced than we imagine. However, if any other species had managed to separate themselves from their environment to the point where they believed that they existed independently from their immediate world and were able to move around in an artificial space-time matrix, then it is absolutely inevitable that they would have gone down the same route as the human race. The key is having a sense of self awareness, something which we humans are almost unable to imagine living without. This sense is part of our DNA, and is the principal reason that we just can't see the paradoxical nature of our lives.

Of course, animals are affected by what has happened in the past and will also view objects and beings as having some sort of permanence, but their reaction is likely to be more immediate and instinctive. If, for example, a dog meets another dog that had previously attacked it, it is very likely to have an impact on its behaviour. However, this is not the same thing as making a moral judgement about it. It is an immediate reaction caused by previous experience, and is part of a process which sentient beings constantly use to better master their environment and aid survival. I am no expert on animal behaviour, and it may well be that some species, e.g. dolphins or chimpanzees, are very advanced; however, this has no bearing on the human condition. For if,

4. MORALITY

like us, they had egos which felt constantly threatened by the fluidity and impermanence of life, they would inevitably behave like us.

Morality, therefore, is not just a set of rules that through genetic inheritance and learnt behaviour we automatically accept as the basis for our actions, but rather a set of highly complex abstract concepts, which we can choose to observe or not. Along with all the other parameters I have mentioned, it is also one of the principal determinants of our individuality. How we view our own behaviour in the context of our moral beliefs is a very important part of our identity and of course how we think other people view us. As I discussed in my chapter on the individual, our notion of self is both incredibly complex and highly fluid, and morality both underpins and interacts with this process in a multitude of ways. We have our moral beliefs or lack of them, a sense of how we should behave even though we don't, a feeling of guilt for not behaving as we would wish to, an awareness of what we believe other people think about us, moral judgements about all the people we know, and often a sense of guilt about having wrongly judged other people. Furthermore, our urges and desires are often in conflict with our moral sense, leading to all kinds of internal conflicts which may lead us to feel guilty and even more insecure. For this reason, morality cannot simply be viewed as a benign and inevitable part of human life but rather one of the factors which actually aggravates the human condition. As incredible as it may seem, morality because it causes us to judge ourselves and others leads to greater insecurity and ultimately suffering. Your immediate reaction might well be, hang on a minute, without morality our world would be a thousand times worse! Oddly enough, whether this is the case or not is completely beside the point, because there is no choice involved. The creation and development of our artificial universe must inevitably lead to where we are today. Morals are not imposed on us by others, but are an intrinsic part of our function as human beings. As with money, they also play a role in our endless quest to shore up our sense of self in the face of relentless evidence that we don't actually exist in the way we believe. In this process everything is viewed in relation to how we feel. Simply put, if we believe we have done a good thing this will generally lead us to have pleasant sensations, and conversely if we feel we are behaving badly we are likely to feel guilty. However, this process is clearly much more complex than that and involves comparing ourselves to others, wishing to be other than we are, and a multitude of other desires, fears and feelings. Everything we do is in relation to our ego and as a result we constantly seek to appease our sense of insecurity and view everything through this lens. This is why ultimately people can do as much good as they humanly can, but it will not alter the fundamental issue at the heart of our condition which is our illusory separation from our immediate environment. However good we feel about ourselves, it cannot stop us doubting our existence and the validity of the self.

4. MORALITY

Furthermore, our behaviour is often highly contradictory, which can be very difficult to accept. I was frequently puzzled as a child by people who devoted themselves to good causes but behaved very badly to their nearest and dearest. This type of behaviour is extremely common, and as we all know no one is perfect or at least not from a moral perspective. The reality is that morals are not some set-in-stone rules which keep us all on the straight and narrow, but rather a complex and fluid set of abstract guidelines which reflect our fractured and contradictory sense of self. So although on the surface moral beliefs seem to be a force for good in society compared to, say, money, which many people would be happy to label as the source of all evil, the reality is quite different. Both are attempts to compensate for the insecurity of our existence and both are not only sadly fated to fail but also to actually aggravate the situation.

Hitler's Germany and Stalin's Russia are commonly viewed as situations where the normal moral order broke down with the resulting catastrophic consequences. I wouldn't disagree that life in today's democratic countries is incomparably better than it was under such murderous and barbaric regimes; however, I do not think one can view this as reason to celebrate the triumph of morality. As I mentioned in the introduction, if humankind had really moved on from the horrors of the Second World War, there would have been no Chinese Cultural Revolution, or Yugoslavian and Rwandan genocides.

However, this does not stop us believing in the necessity of a moral base and an enormous part of a child's upbringing is concerned with this. We constantly hear the necessity of giving our children strong morals to help them lead happy and fulfilled lives. If we were not to do this as parents, our children would indeed find life very hard, as in order to socialise successfully and get ahead in our world, you need to behave in what society regards as an acceptable manner. This requires you to understand what the acceptable limits of behaviour are and where you are going to start seriously stepping on other people's toes. This aspect of morality is, of course, much closer to the learning process that animals go through, but is nevertheless hugely complicated by our illusory sense of self and the highly complex artificial world we live in. Furthermore, humans, unlike animals, do not simply accept these rules (or ignore them) without questioning, but absorb them into their developing and incredibly complex sense of self. How we are brought up has a huge influence on who we are and the concepts of right and wrong, good and evil are at the very core of the process. As we grow up we gradually learn that we are responsible for our actions and that we are expected to be able to judge whether what we do is right or wrong. Whilst animals also learn what is acceptable and unacceptable, they do so on the basis of immediate consequences. For them it is simply another aspect of the universal learning process which all intelligent life on earth uses to learn and develop.

4. MORALITY

Although my dog knows when I catch him on the sofa that he has done something wrong, I very much doubt he feels guilty about it or at least if he does it will be an immediate feeling which he will forget almost immediately. However, for us humans, learning about right and wrong is an essential part of a child's upbringing and it is no surprise to me that childhood, especially at key moments such as the early teens, can be very difficult. It is difficult enough as an adult to maintain the illusion of individuality; however, to actually to go through the process of building it up in the face of so many changes, both internal and external, is a huge challenge. As I have already tried to explain, the world we live in, based on an artificial concept of time and space, is vast, complex and pretty incomprehensible. If anything, this situation is only becoming more extreme the more our society becomes fragmented and separated from our immediate world. To begin to make sense of this world and your place in it, especially when you are beginning to spread your wings and become more independent of your parents, is no easy task. In situations where family life is dysfunctional and parents are unable to support their children, or even worse aggravate their children's insecurity through psychological or even physical violence, children, especially if they are more vulnerable, are likely to suffer very badly.

If morality were set in stone, learning about it would be relatively straightforward, but what makes it even more difficult to live with, is its endless diversity and inherently contradictory nature. We are not, of course, surprised that the moral codes of the Ancient Egyptians or the Aztecs do not have much in common with those of a modern democratic state.(For the Aztecs, human sacrifice including the sacrifice of children were important religious rituals.) However, differences between moral positions within society and even between different individuals are much more difficult to understand and deal with. A child may have parents with very rigid moral views, which are in obvious contrast to those of their friends, or there may be a big difference between the moralities of each parent. Frequently you also find that parents will say one thing but do another, and also change the rules depending on their mood. I have frequently come across parents who are very relaxed and indulgent with their children, but then freak out at them regularly because they can't cope with their behaviour. This is not a book about child psychology and I am certainly no expert; however, I do know that children must find it very difficult to make sense of a world, which is made up of endless shifting shades of grey.

What makes this even more difficult is that, unlike with animals, parents cannot simply restrict themselves to teaching their children how to behave in the immediacy of an event, but must give them general ground rules for behaviour. Thus, moral teaching provides general abstract rules about how to behave in a variety of situations. However, such rules are often in stark contrast to what you can actually observe happening. In

4. MORALITY

my own childhood I never forget the contrast between the religious and moral teaching I received and the behaviour which I observed around me, especially in my family. As I have said in the introduction, from a very young age I have been badly affected by the pain and suffering I observed in the world and I was acutely aware that it was in direct contradiction to the moral world I was being educated in. For animals, behavioural codes make sense and work, but for us they are abstract concepts which are taught but largely ignored. Children are not stupid and can see this with the result that they are never going to feel very secure.

As I keep on saying, our world goes way beyond our immediate environment, to the limits of our enormous shared reality. Whereas in the case of animals, it is immediate behaviour which is relevant, in the case of us humans, it could be an intention to do something at some point in the future or something which we may have done in the past. Of course, an animal's previous experiences will impact its future interactions; however, this will be an instinctive reaction, based on the same principles as Pavlov's experiment. In the case of humans, we consciously judge behaviour. Furthermore, because we are aware of ourselves as much as we are aware of others, it is not simply a question of being reprimanded by others, but also of judging ourselves. Our consciousness enables us to judge our imaginary selves, according to our moral values and of course any other criteria we choose to apply.

Because human society is so much larger and more complex than that of any animals, its behavioural codes are also inevitably going to be more complex. However, it is human self-awareness which is the key difference between humans and non-humans, and it is because of this that we have a concept of morality as being separate to us. It is this key difference, which creates all of the problems associated with moral judgement. By being separate we can view ourselves in relation to it and are able to judge others and ourselves. The moment we broke free from our environment, and became self-aware, the process of separation began. It is this process which changed a set of unwritten, implicit behavioural guidelines, used by all social beings and determined by a mixture of heredity and environment into the concept of morality. However, this has not been a static process and as our world has gradually become more and more complex, so have the moral codes which accompany it. With the information revolution, which had its roots in the development of printing some 500 years ago, and is now being expanded at an exponential rate via the internet and all its associated developments, our world is becoming unimaginably larger. This is a one-way process, which has a number of facets including a continuous increase in our sense of individuality. The basic paradox which was created when humans first became aware of themselves, has not changed one iota; however, the artificial world, which is the direct result of this awareness, has gradually become more and more complex. The larger our world and the greater

4. MORALITY

our apparent scope of action, the more importance the moral world has taken on.

Today a staggering percentage of our population, especially in the developed world, lives alone, and our interactions reflect this. We increasingly communicate with other people without being physically present, often isolated at our computer terminals. This is the culmination of a long process of separation and individualisation which I have already spoken about in previous chapters. In the moral sphere this has meant a gradual replacement of unwritten rules of behaviour rooted in community and family by individualised rights and abstract moral concepts. I am not trying to wax lyrical about the good old days, and as I have said from the beginning of the book, suffering has been with us from time immemorial. My aim is rather to explain how we ended up here and why, just like individuality itself, morality is fundamentally paradoxical. For example, is it not frequently necessary to decide which of our morals are the most important? If you have been unfaithful to your husband or wife, is it better to lie to them or tell them the truth? By telling them the truth you may be ruining your marriage and having a highly detrimental effect on your children. But by lying you may be compounding a moral transgression you have already committed, i.e. adultery. If the only way you could stop the expansion of horrific dictatorship was by killing its civilians and soldiers, would you feel justified in doing this? This must have been the question on many allied soldiers' minds during the Second World

War. Even if you felt you were doing the right thing, it might not make the actual act of killing any easier. Do you think that it was right for the Americans to drop the atomic bombs on Japan in order to bring a speedy halt to the war? There are valid moral arguments on either side. Our lives are full of moral dilemmas and there is often no easy answer. There are also going to be differences between the morals of different societies both today and at different times in history.

One of the areas where such moral dilemmas abound is in the field of individual rights. I remember an ongoing argument between the Marxists and the liberals in my university's politics department. For the liberals it was enough that rights protected you from such evils as arbitrary imprisonment, discrimination for your racial origins, gender or sexual orientation, whilst the Marxists believed that there is not much point being free of such moral infringements if you didn't have enough to eat! For them, it would be immoral if a society allowed people to live without adequate food, shelter and clothing. Modern western society seems to reflect aspects of both these views, although they can often be in conflict. For example, it may seem immoral to some people that they should pay their hard earned taxes in order for other people to live on public handouts.

Rights and morals are not, of course, exactly the same thing, but do, however, share a common intellectual base. Rights are very much part of how we define individuality and their increasing importance over

4. MORALITY

the last few hundred years has accompanied the rapid individualisation of post-enlightenment society. This process would not, however, make any sense without a moral framework. Rights are in a sense the crystallised and specified guidelines of how individuals both privately and collectively should behave towards each other. However, these rights will always be to some extent conflictual. If you take one of the classic rights, such as the right to free speech, it is often likely to be in conflict with rights which protect sexual orientation, or religious and cultural choice.

A recent example I read about was where a highly religious couple who owned a bed and breakfast tried to refuse to accept a gay couple as guests. The owners felt that their right to live by their religion, which included a moral opposition to homosexuality, should enable them to refuse to accept practising homosexuals as guests. Of course, the position of the gay couple was quite the opposite and they simply felt that their right to be treated as equal to heterosexuals was being violated. These kinds of situations arise constantly and frequently end up in the courts. Another example of this kind of conflict is the banning by the French government of the wearing of full-face veils in public places. To many French people, having women walking around with their faces covered is an affront to the rights of women and their moral and legal equality to men, whilst to many of the women who are banned from dressing this way, the ban is viewed as an affront to their religious freedom and individual rights.

Another area which always causes a great deal of controversy, and where morality and rights are frequently in conflict, is abortion. In this situation the right to life of the unborn child is pitted directly against the wish of the mother not to carry the baby to term. Both points of view can be understood, yet it is almost inconceivable that they can be reconciled! The result is conflict, not only between those whose opinions are opposed but also potentially within mothers whose belief that they have a right to abort does not necessarily mean they are guilt-free. This is quite likely to make them feel bad about themselves, further weakening their sense of individuality.

People often talk about the importance of having a sense of self-worth and there are numerous psychological techniques to try and help us achieve this. However, although such techniques may be useful in helping people cope, it is impossible to change the fundamental paradox which creates the problems in the first place. As human society has evolved, morality, just like money, has gradually developed and become more complex. It has accompanied the gradual expansion of the human world into time and space, and now permeates every aspect of our existence in various guises, mostly via our legal systems but also through moral conventions. In the last chapter I tried to explain how property and its principal manifestation, money, were the unsurprising results of our constant search to reassure ourselves of our existence as individuals. There are, of course, many other facets of this process, some of which I

4. MORALITY

mentioned in my chapter on individuality. The result is human behaviour that is often incomprehensible and consequently very difficult to cope with. For most people, the violence, destruction, pain and suffering which surrounds them has to be made sense of in some way or other. This not only makes life easier to cope with, but it can also give us the hope that there is potential for improvement. The basis of this process is having a sense of right or wrong, or good and bad. These are the measuring rods we use to judge the behaviour of ourselves and those around us. Furthermore, they are the basis of our moral codes which provide the guidelines of socially acceptable behaviour.

However, morality, if it were simply a set of rules which enabled people to live and thrive as social animals, would not fulfil a much more fundamental human need. This is to be able to separate themselves from what they see as bad or the cause of suffering. It's bad enough to spend your time trying to convince yourself that you exist as a fixed individual in the face of the endless stream of evidence to the contrary, without having to admit that this struggle you are going through causes immeasurable pain and suffering. Our egos are never going to admit that they are the cause of our problems and we are therefore going to come up with an alternative scenario which will enable us to explain our situation. This is why we created the idea of "Good and Evil" as independent entities, which society in general accepts as autonomous forces which shape our world. This view is personified, at least in the

Christian tradition, in the difference between the forces of good represented by "God" and the forces of evil represented by the "Devil". This is vividly represented in the depictions of heaven and hell found in medieval religious art. All that is regarded as bad and related to suffering is put into hell, and everything good and spiritually pure is put in heaven. Although in recent times, at least in Western civilisation, the religious aspect of this point of view has faded away, the basic mechanism remains intact. You still regularly hear of people, organisations and regimes being branded as evil. Not so long ago the US labelled a group of countries including Iran and North Korea as the "axis of evil"! Of course, you can say that this statement was just politics, but it would have fallen on deaf ears if people did not readily recognise the basic process at work.

What is going on here is an externalisation of the moral struggles we all face on a regular basis. Being a conscious individual is an extremely difficult place to be, partly because as I have already pointed out we constantly doubt our existence, and are prepared to go to extraordinary lengths to persuade ourselves that we do actually exist. However, this situation is compounded a thousand-fold, because we are aware of our thoughts and our actions and will feel bad about it. We seem to be caught in a trap between the impulses which lead us to cause pain and suffering to ourselves and those around us, and the desire to feel good about ourselves. By externalising this struggle, we can unload some of the responsibility and place our faith in forces which are greater than us. However, we do not restrict ourselves to viewing these forces as purely abstract, and will often personify these concepts through individuals or groups, real or imagined. As I have already mentioned, the most basic of these "incarnations" are "God and the Devil"; however, these labels are also applied to individuals and groups of people. Whenever you hear appalling cases of people being unimaginably cruel to others, they will often be described as "evil people". This language is often used to describe paedophiles and other people who engage in acts that society, as a whole, views as totally unacceptable. This same approach is used with brutal dictators and repressive regimes. It makes it possible for us to live in our world without wanting to commit a mass collective suicide.

In the case of President's Bush "axis of evil", these concepts are being used as a justification for specific types of behaviour, i.e. US government actions to apparently fight or at least contain these forces for evil. This kind of labelling has been used since time immemorial to further the interests of certain groups at the expense of others. In Hitler's Germany the communists and Jews were given the role of bogeymen, whilst in more recent times Islamic extremists incarnated in Osama Bin Laden have played the same role. It is part of exactly the same process that we use to create and maintain our identity. The advantage of Good and Evil over, say, nationality is that believing that you are part of the forces for good whilst externalising all the bad in your life into whatever form you choose provides an enormous boost to the ego. Not only do you exist but your life has a purpose, whilst all the bad things that go on and make your life hard are the fault of other people or even shadowy and hidden forces. It really is a supreme psychological Houdini act!

Furthermore, in order to be able to cope, we need to be able to explain, understand and of course hope that there is potential for improvement. This is why we have developed complex moral codes and laws backed up by legal systems. If human behaviour was always exemplary and our world was filled with happiness and kindness, we would clearly not feel it necessary to create these systems. There appear to be two principal aspects to this process, both of which are, of course, completely interconnected. The first is having a concept of good and evil in order to make it possible for us to make sense of human behaviour, and the second is a set of morals or behavioural codes which help guide people in their behaviour.

Because we are aware of morality as a set of abstract concepts, we need to have an intellectual basis for it. This is why we spend so much time trying to teach our children the difference between right and wrong. The reason that stealing is not considered to be normal or acceptable behaviour is not that people are afraid of getting punished, but rather that they believe that it is wrong. Clearly, the underlying reason is that stealing undermines our economic and social systems; however, this is not something that is ever really talked about.

4. MORALITY

Stealing is wrong, bad or evil, and that is why we shouldn't do it. In the case of a dog, you can train them to not steal, but you will not need to explain to them why this should be the case. In the case of humans, the process is quite a bit more complicated, which is why it is so useful to have good and evil as independent abstract concepts. This is perhaps why children's stories often have very strong characters representing these two opposing concepts. Witches, man-eating giants, wolves and innumerable other wicked characters pepper the pages of children's stories. At the age of around 4-5, I remember having a recurring nightmare about an evil witch that came in through my bedroom window to take me away. I doubt I am the only child who has had such experiences and it must be part of the way children absorb the concepts of good and bad into their psyche. Once these notions are established, then it is far easier to introduce morality which will always be in relation to these fundamental concepts. If you think about it, all morals, whether they concern apparently trivial or very serious behaviour, function on this basis. Of course, on a daily basis we are not aware of this at all, and we just accept the fact that certain things can be classified as good and others as bad.

Yet even if you take what many people might consider to be the ultimate evil act – killing – it quickly becomes apparent our normal way of viewing it is simply a convenient illusion. This is most obviously illustrated by the fact that certain types of killing are absolutely fine. A significant part of the training that soldiers receive is to put them in a state of mind where they are able to kill others, and in general the public clearly accepts that killing in this context is not evil. As a rule, we are thankful for what our soldiers do and we accept killing as a necessary part of their job. The same can be said for anti-terrorist police and any other government agents whose work is considered to be beneficial to our society as a whole.

Another very significant example is the death penalty. In the US, many of the people who support this form of punishment have very strong moral and religious beliefs, based on a concept of good and evil, including of course "thou shalt not kill". Yet this does not stop them believing very strongly that those who commit certain crimes should be killed. The name might have been changed to "executed" but killing is definitely what is going on.

In effect what is happening is that we are seeing those shades of grey beginning to creep into the situation. It is not killing per se which is considered to be bad, but only the fact that it is carried out under certain circumstances. This is why we have different words to describe killing in a variety of situations, i.e. murder, execution, manslaughter, collateral damage, take-out etc. As is hopefully becoming clear, we do not have a problem with killing another human being, but rather with the fact that some types of killing upset the functioning of our society. None of us would want it to be acceptable to kill people at random, because we

4. MORALITY

would all feel incredibly insecure, yet we are mostly perfectly happy for people to be killed if they are perceived to be threatening us.

You can see the same pattern with regard to another of the major activities which almost all societies regard as wrong: stealing. It has always struck me as very bizarre, that certain types of theft are considered to be much worse than others, even though the amount stolen may be far less. So, for example, if I was to steal some goods from a shop, maybe some jewellery or an expensive watch, I would be in far greater trouble than if I failed to declare some revenue to the 'taxman'. In fact, it is widely accepted that white collar crime is subject to lesser punishment than straight up theft.

Furthermore, a lot of companies – with banks being a very good example – engage in activities which many people would regard as being theft in all but name. There was a recent scandal in the UK where banks were taken to court and forced to reimburse huge amounts of money to customers who had had products miss-sold to them. If people have had money returned to them, it suggests to me that money was taken off them illegally, which in plain English means money was stolen off them. The fact that they might have agreed to something doesn't make any difference as they were not given the full facts. However, the euphemism used is "mis-selling" in order to distinguish it from good old-fashioned theft. So once again an act which most of us believe can clearly be labelled as wrong, is viewed differently in different circumstances.

This same process can be seen to be at work with almost all apparently fixed moral rules. Lying is a case in point and it is certainly something that most parents feel their children should simply not do. In fact, you often hear parents say that the lying was worse than the actual misdemeanour committed. Yet it is clear that lying is a completely normal aspect of the functioning of our society and almost no one is free from this tendency. Once again, the basic idea is that if everyone lied, you would not be able to trust anyone and it would become very difficult for society to function effectively. We know, however, that almost everyone presents situations in a way which makes them look as good as possible and this can vary from placing particular emphasis on certain aspects of what you are claiming, to simple invention. Once again it is possible to see this in the workings of our consumer society. If we come back to the "mis-selling" scandal of the banks, in order to be able to persuade people to part with their money, they had to effectively lie to their customers or at least not tell them the whole truth. This type of behaviour is so ubiquitous in our society that we basically expect certain types of people, for example politicians, to distort the truth or in plain English "tell lies". The same is clearly the case in journalism, where facts are presented in such a way that the event which is being reported on is distorted out of all recognition. On the several occasions when I have directly experienced

4. MORALITY

journalism, I have been amazed by what was written, as it seemed to bear almost no resemblance to what happened. This was not only a question of interpretation but of plain facts, such as age, nationality and the place where the event took place. In these cases, there was no reason for this besides sloppy journalism, but in many situations it is more about selling the news or perhaps the political agenda of the paper.

What makes this situation even more complex is that in many cases "the truth" is actually quite nebulous, which is why it is possible to present an event in two or more completely different ways. It is generally believed that "facts" are concrete events or situations which are not dependent on anyone's point of view. However, it seems that even "facts" appear to change according to where you are standing. If you ask almost anyone who has been involved in an accident or an event which later on people tried to reconstruct, it is very likely that people had different recollections of what actually went on. This is because our view of the world is unique and is coloured by the dynamic construction which is our individuality. As a result, we observe the world around us through the lens of our conditioning and our particular stage in life.

A good example would be the difference in the way a child and an adult might describe the same person. To a child, if that person is an adult, their notion of size and age is likely to be quite different to that of another adult. The child is also likely to view what that person is actually doing completely differently to adults, because they are unlikely to share the same pre-conceptions or interpretation of what they have seen. Just as with language and culture, the closer people are in terms of all the parameters which make up their individuality, the more likely they are to view things in a similar way. The result is that it can often be very difficult to establish precisely what the truth is, and consequently to prove with any degree of certainty that someone has lied.

This is clearly illustrated by the field of statistics, which at least on the surface should enable us to establish the actual state or truth of a situation. If you take "Global warming", for example, most of us accept that the theory must be based on hard evidence and is therefore unquestionable. However, a scandal known as "Climate gate" which erupted over some hacked emails that were sent by scientists from the University of East Anglia seems to blow this point of view out of the water. These scientists appeared to be deliberately ignoring evidence which did not back up their theory. This is why it is possible to not only argue almost anything but to back up the argument with hard facts. Because our illusory world is so huge and complex, you are able to pick and choose the version of reality you wish to present.

In order for any kind of moral judgement to function, it is, of course, absolutely vital for there to be a measure of agreement, and this will depend on there being enough common ground in order to produce a story which

4. MORALITY

people are prepared to accept. However, the risk, and frequently the reality, is that events are interpreted to suit the needs of a person or a group of people. This is why "fairness" is very hard to come by! In the 2011 London riots, some rioters were given sentences which were completely disproportionate to the offences committed. The idea was to make an example so that people think twice about behaving in this way again. So, a decision which at least in theory was based on one of the tenets of a moral code: though shalt not steal, was in fact based on the imperative of restoring social order and the functioning of the economy. This same process repeats itself endlessly whether it is in the family, school, work or greater civic environment. Unfortunately, it is highly detrimental to the quality of our lives as moral judgements are often used to boost our egos at the expense of others. We all know of times when we are made to feel incredibly small by a teacher, or another person in authority who has accused us of a moral transgression. Both my sister and wife went to convent schools and have horrific stories of being sarcastically put down and humiliated by nuns. This is the kind of experience which unfortunately many people across the world have suffered and continue to suffer as we speak. I am certainly not saying that all nuns are guilty of this behaviour, nor that it only exists in convent schools, but rather that it is an example of the way morality is used to boost our sense of individuality, often at the expense of others.

This kind of behaviour can become extreme, and is often associated with a desire to "cleanse" society, from its ills. A horrific example in the relatively recent past was the "Khmer Rouge revolution" in Cambodia. This revolution, which was based on an ideological attempt to cleanse society and start anew, quickly ended up in a horrific dictatorship which caused the death and suffering of millions of people. Its theoretical basis was a Maoist form of communism, which aimed to get rid of the evils of capitalism, religion, class and colonialism. Society was to be cleansed of all that made it bad so that it could start anew, the slate wiped clean. The result as we all know was a disaster in which hundreds of thousands, possibly even millions died. This was in effect a revolution in moral extremism, which inevitably ended up causing suffering many times worse than the ills it was supposed to cure. Sadly, it is far from being the only example of this kind of behaviour, as is exemplified by numerous revolutions which have ended up causing horrific death and suffering.

So not only are our morals nebulous and open to interpretation depending on the agenda we might have at any particular time, but even the behaviour which these morals are supposed to be able to judge, are not fixed and obvious in the way we imagine. What they enable us to do, however, is convince ourselves of the validity and worth of our lives and societies, which in consequence reinforces our notion of individual existence. The entire edifice is a creation which we use to reassure ourselves of our own existence and to help

4. MORALITY

shape our society in the direction we believe best suits us. The result is twofold: we are even more convinced of the validity and rationality of our world whilst at the same time being made ever more vulnerable to the suffering which inevitably follows.

5. RELIGION

Religion has played a central role in human life for thousands of years, although its exact form has varied enormously both over time and with different cultures. As I clearly stated at the beginning of this book, I am not trying to explain specific human behaviour and this is also true with regard to religion. What I want to explore in this chapter is what it is about the human situation that brings religion into existence and the role it plays in helping us deal with the paradoxes which make up our lives. As with other aspects of life, there will be differences in the way people approach religion and the way in which it fulfils their needs. However, there are some common threads which allow one to group together a range of belief systems under that heading. As I illustrated in previous chapters, there are a variety of different ways that we can try to deal with the paradoxical nature of our existence. Money and all it represents in terms of our search for psychological stability is one way that humans try to deal with the ephemeral nature of life. Yet it is clear that there are

5. RELIGION

aspects of our lives where the ownership of material goods or social status is simply not going to be of much use.

In this chapter I am going to focus on the organised religions of the last few thousand years. It is likely that some kind of belief in stories or forces that help explain the mysteries and uncertainties of life have been around for far longer than that. However, at some point religion started creating sophisticated scenarios to deal with the issue of life after death. Clearly, the more sophisticated our world has become, the greater the challenge religion has faced to shore up our individuality in the face of ageing, disability, death and uncertainty.

By becoming aware of ourselves as individuals, separate from our immediate environment, and by living in a constructed space-time matrix where we are able to imagine ourselves in a different place and time, we have become acutely aware of our own mortality. This is something that is simply impossible to ignore and which to some extent completely undermines all the efforts that we make to give our lives meaning. What is the use of spending your life striving to improve your lot when at the end of all this effort you will simply disappear? Striving to create and maintain our individuality in the face of all the challenges which can so easily shatter it, is very hard work indeed and for it all just to disappear in a puff of smoke is for many people simply intolerable. In the Catholic Church which I was brought up in, it is clear that death and what happens after it plays an absolutely central role. The very core of the Christian tradition is based on the death and the later resurrection of Christ, and this is celebrated in every church service. Furthermore, it is clear that how you live your life will have a direct impact on what happens to you after death. If you are good you will go to heaven, and will live in paradise free of all pain and suffering, but if you are a sinner, you will at the very least have to spend some time in Purgatory, where you will serve out your time in order to atone for your sins before being admitted to heaven. Last but certainly not least, there is hell, where those who fully embraced evil will rot for eternity. I am not sure if any modern day churches actually still talk of people going to hell, but the concept of hell is still very much alive and well.

As far as I know, dealing with the issue of death is at the very basis of every religion that exists or probably has ever existed. Whilst Christianity, and as I understand it, the other great monotheistic religions see life after death as essentially being about judgement and redemption of the soul, many others including Buddhism and Hinduism use the concept of reincarnation. In this scenario individuals go through a series of lives with their current existence being just one of the many. In some traditions including that of the Ancient Greeks it is possible to be reincarnated into a totally different form, i.e. an animal. Although there are obviously major differences between the ideologies of these two approaches, there is one fundamental similarity: life does not stop with death. What makes this belief

5. RELIGION

possible is the dividing up of people into different parts. From this perspective it is not possible to view ourselves as a single indivisible unit otherwise it would be impossible to argue that once the physical side had died something else continues to exist. In the western tradition we divide people up into three parts: the physical, mental and spiritual. The spiritual side of our existence is represented by the soul, and it is this aspect of our existence that will continue to exist after death. It is the soul that will leave the body and be judged for the actions of the person during their lifetime. In order for the soul to be able to fulfil this role it must, however, have one fundamental attribute which the other aspects of our existence clearly lack: immortality. In addition, the soul must represent our "essence" or the real "you" because as we all know our physical and mental sides are in a continuous state of change. In this way we are reassured that even though we are constantly changing and then die, there is a constant me that is immortal. This is, of course, an absolutely enormous boost to our ego that is constantly worried about the threat of annihilation, both in terms of its current existence, which as I have already pointed out is entirely illusory, and of course with regards to death, which will ensure its annihilation regardless of what it does. If you believe that there is a constant indestructible me represented by the soul, your ego is going to feel an awful lot safer. It is going to make facing up to ageing, trauma and all the other problems we face in life much easier to deal with and, most important of all, it means we can be reassured that we will not disappear after death.

Although I am less familiar with Buddhism and Hinduism, and I understand that they do not have the same concept of the soul as in the Christian tradition, it is clear that if someone is going to be reincarnated into a different person, there has to be an essence of that person which assumes another identity in their next life. Just as with Christianity, there is "something" which is immortal and largely unchangeable about ourselves which deals with the issues of constant change and death. The concept of reincarnation is an extremely old one, which appears to have originated with the aboriginal tribes of the sub-Indian continent, who passed it on to the Indo-Aryans around 2500 BC. It also existed in the Ancient Greek civilisation, which might possibly have been influenced by Indian thinking. The important point, however, is that very early on man used the concept of reincarnation (this word was only invented in the 19th century and is a general heading for a family of traditions), in order to deal with the most basic problems posed by his illusory individuality: "if I am an individual how can I define the real me?" and "if I exist as an independent identity, how can I possibly cease to exist when I die?". The premise for this approach which has not changed one iota since man first started observing himself, is that we are individual beings. Once you take up this position and make it the basis of your existence, you create a paradox which requires extraordinary artifice to explain and deal with. This is the basis for the various solutions that religions have developed and refined to both explain death and make it easier to cope with.

5. RELIGION

However, if the solution works and makes our lives better, what is the problem with it? What on earth could be the harm in believing that our lives will continue either as a reincarnation or as a soul residing in Paradise? Perhaps the most obvious problem with believing in life after death is that by reinforcing our faith in our individuality and existence, it strengthens our ego and makes our potential for suffering greater. By enabling us to believe that there is an indissoluble essence to our existence which will continue to exist after our death, it anchors us ever more firmly in our illusory world and makes our ego larger and ever more determined to prove its importance. This is likely to feed and encourage the other mechanisms we use to strengthen our ego, such as the accumulation of material goods, social status and morality. Because of this, people will be much more easily able to engage in activities which will ultimately harm others in the belief that they are helping themselves.

You might, of course, imagine that the moral aspect of their religion would counterbalance this tendency. Yet the evidence doesn't seem to support this view as in addition to enabling us to believe that we will continue to exist after death, religion also provides a mechanism by which people are able to convince themselves that because they are abiding by the rules they are behaving rightly. If you take early capitalism in Britain as an example, most of the early factory owners, bankers, mine owners etc. were strong Christian believers, often non-conformist Protestants (i.e. Quakers, Baptists etc.). This type of Protestantism was very much about individualism, personal moral responsibility and a direct relationship with God. They had a strong belief in hard work, thrift and high moral standards, and as long as they felt that they were adhering to the tenets of their religion, they probably found it a lot easier to brush the exploitation of their workforces under the table. Indeed, the Victorian period, which was a very active one from a religious and moral perspective, was also rife with poverty and exploitation. It was a world in which churchgoing and strong moral values lived alongside child labour, slums and very high levels of prostitution. This does not mean that there were not Christians of all faiths who dedicated themselves to alleviating the lot of the poor and oppressed, but rather that religion, by enabling people to feel morally righteous, meant that they could feel good about themselves and what they were doing, simply by convincing themselves that they were being good Christians. One must also not forget that Marx described religion as "the opium of the people" and it is clear that the Christian message can also work very well in convincing the poor and downtrodden that despite what they have to put up with in this life, they will be rewarded in the next by going to heaven. The Church of England embarked on a huge church building programme during the 19th century specifically to try and pacify the urban poor, who the establishment believed posed a threat to the stability of society.

5. RELIGION

Interestingly enough, this belief in a continued existence after death is not restricted to organised religion but plays a very large part in the animist beliefs which predated the great religions. They not only continue to influence many religious beliefs but still exist independently in many parts of the world today including Africa. My understanding is animists see the world as essentially made up of spirits that are found in animals, plants and of course humans. These spirits have different characters, roles and can be either benevolent or malevolent and their behaviour provides the rationale and explanation for the vagaries of human life. So, for example, if the harvest fails it is because a particular spirit is displeased most probably by someone or some people's actions. In order to try and placate them and ensure that life goes smoothly, spirits are often worshipped through prayer and sacrifice. As with religion, life is not perceived to stop at death and the dead are frequently revered. In order to keep contact with these spirits, many people keep the bones of their ancestors nearby. Whilst animism in all its varied forms might enable those who live by it, to have a rationale for the paradoxes of existence, just as in the case of organised religion, the side effects can be very painful. Innocent people can easily end up being blamed for causing other people's misfortunes, and can suffer badly because of it, even to the point of being killed. Sadly, as with all human activity, people will use religious or spiritual beliefs to gain power and achieve various social and economic goals to the detriment of others.

Because religion can play such an essential role in the make-up of our individuality, people can go to extreme lengths to defend it. As history has shown, this has included killing, torturing and even being prepared to die defending it. This is made possible because of the conviction that these actions are somehow morally righteous and that the perpetrators will end up in heaven because of them. This is supposed to be the case for the suicide bombers who blow themselves up in the name of god. There are also numerous examples of people being prepared to fight wars partly because they believed participating in them would be good for their souls. There is the example of the Crusades, where Christian knights and their followers waged a series of campaigns over several hundred years in order to restore access for Christians to the Holy Land, which was ruled by the Ottoman Empire. Those that participated were granted "plenary indulgences" or complete forgiveness for their sins by the Pope, which meant that they could go to their deaths knowing they would go straight to heaven. This would have made participating in a project which caused immeasurable suffering much easier. They were in effect licensed to rape and pillage by the Church who told them that they were doing it in the name of Christ and would go straight to heaven as a result!

So, there are a variety of different traditions, which although very different all share the aim of convincing us that life continues after death. All of them inevitably strengthen the ego, and make whatever reality you have constructed more real. One of the associated aspects of

5. RELIGION

this process is the interplay these belief systems have with morality. In the case of the Christian tradition, the fact that you are going to be judged for your behaviour during your life when you die is likely to hugely strengthen the hold of morality on believers. Indeed, until relatively recently morality has very much been the domain of religion. In Christianity and Judaism, the fundamental moral precepts were laid down in the Ten Commandments and they continue to be the basis of our moral world. For Christians and Jews, life on Earth is very much seen as a test where our job is to resist temptation and prove ourselves worthy of God's love, with life in heaven being the reward. The story of Adam and Eve where the Serpent (a symbol for Evil) tricks Eve into taking a bite from the apple of the tree of knowledge who then persuades Adam to taste it, perfectly illustrates this point. By giving in to Evil and disobeying God, man has ended up suffering. Although on Earth, tainted as we are by original sin, we cannot hope to re-enter paradise, if we behave during our lives and resist the temptation of sinning, we will do well at the final judgement, going swiftly to heaven where we will live in bliss for ever more. One can see that this is a brilliant solution to two of the fundamental issues we face as human beings: the fact that we are all going to die, and the fact that our lives are full of suffering. In the Christian tradition we are assured that we, or at least the core aspect of our being represented by the soul, will continue to live after death, and furthermore if we behave well on Earth, the afterlife will be one without pain and suffering. No wonder this message has been so popular!

Unfortunately, although it may be a brilliant intellectual solution to the fundamental issues we face as human beings, it doesn't actually resolve the problem. The reality of living an illusory individuality is not going to be helped by clever theories which help explain the problems caused by our paradoxical situation. One of the principal purposes of the story of Adam and Eve is to explain why there is pain and suffering in this world and to propose a solution which unfortunately will only take effect in the afterlife. From a sales perspective you can't really do a better job, as it manages to neatly explain why we are in a terrible mess as well as giving us a solution whose effectiveness can never really be judged as it only comes into effect in the afterlife. Furthermore, although the origins of Christianity may well have been rooted in a desire to change the world for the better, as it gradually became the dominant religion it metamorphosed into a tool for social control and material advancement.

In the European medieval period, life was not only much more local but also very fragile. People's lives, their families and communities were at constant risk from illness, famine and war. Science in its modern form didn't exist, and just as in the case of the animists there was no rationale for what happened to you other than the will of external forces represented by God or the Devil. In this situation people tended to ascribe what

5. RELIGION

happened to them as related to what they or others had done or even thought. This was a world in which the notion of the devil was a very real one indeed, and people were frequently accused of being his agent. This was very much the root of the witch hunts which plagued late medieval Europe and resulted in the torture and death of hundreds of thousands of people, most of whom were women. These hunts were very much initiated by the Christian church and as with every other type of persecution that has taken place in the history of the human race, they must have been rooted in the lust for power, money and domination. In this way a belief system which at its origins was supposed to alleviate human suffering and reassure people that they would not only survive death but would find themselves in a land free of pain and suffering, ended up being used to persecute innocent people.

It is currently popular to believe that eastern religions or "belief systems" such as Buddhism are free of such moral judgments and their potentially horrific effects. Yet in Buddhist doctrine, there is definitely a sense of morality expressed by the concept of "Good Conduct". This morality may not, as in Christianity, have been dictated by God, but it is nevertheless about being a good Buddhist, and just as in the case of Christianity it will either boost your ego if you feel you are on the right path, or it will dent your self-esteem if you feel you are failing. Furthermore, as with Christianity, your behaviour in this life will have an influence on your next, via the agency of Karma. As I understand it, Karma is based on the law of cause and effect with as a basic precept the saying "what you sow is what you reap". If you behave badly, those actions will come back and affect you at some point in the future and even possibly in another life; however, if you behave well you will be rewarded at some time in the future. The important points to make are the following: just as in Christianity Buddhism enables us to believe that we continue to exist after death, and that our actions in this life will have an impact not only in this life but also in the next. If we behave well our next life will be a better one, and it is also possible to be released entirely from the endless pain and suffering we encounter in this world. Pain and suffering are not as in the Western traditions explained by the existence of an outside malign force in the shape of the devil, but rather are the result of our own actions (which come from our ego-centric makeup). Although there are Buddhists who focus on dissolving the ego, the vast majority are caught in the same ego trap as everyone else, and their religion only worsens the problem. Even in a process whose very raison d'être was the dissolution of the ego, the ego ruled supreme. So, it is inevitable that people going about their daily lives will use Buddhism to boost their individuality, leading as with all other ego boosting activities to more pain and suffering. By believing that they can improve their lot through their actions in this life and the next, they are crystallising the illusion of individuality. I have almost no knowledge of the history of Buddhism from a social and economic perspective, but I am in no doubt that, just as with Christianity, Buddhism has at

5. RELIGION

times been used as an excuse to gain money, power and prestige at the expense of other people.

By solving the most fundamental problems that we face as human beings on Earth, i.e. endless suffering, ageing and death, religion can gain an extraordinary hold over its believers. As I have already spoken about, it quickly becomes an essential part of people's identity and believers can easily feel threatened by the fact that there are those who don't have the same religion. Indeed, it is almost undeniable that of all the different facets which make up our identity, religion is the one which seems to have caused the most pain and suffering. What is particularly strange is that the most basic purpose of religion is to save us from suffering and death. Christianity at its origin is about loving thy neighbour, forgiveness, not killing, rejecting the pursuit of wealth and a host of other moral codes whose aim is to reduce suffering by challenging the ego's lust to dominate and pursue self-gratification. One would have thought that by living the Christian message life on Earth would be a thousand times better than without it. Yet the evidence seems to suggest quite the opposite! Christianity seems, in fact, to have worsened the human condition one thousand-fold. From the crusades, to the inquisition, via the burning of witches, the examples of human suffering resulting from religious conviction are endless. I will never forget writing an essay at university on the 30 years war, which was a 17th century religious conflict between the Protestants and Catholics, mostly fought in Germany. During the war, about half of the entire built environment of Germany was destroyed. This is a scale of destruction that is simply unimaginable, particularly when one considers that when a town was captured by the other side, it was not unusual for every man, woman and child to be killed, often in a horrific manner. If this was not enough, one third of the productive agricultural land was put out of use, often by putting salt into the soil. The result was clearly catastrophic with widescale famines as the inevitable result. Now you might say that religion was merely the excuse for this carnage, which was actually economic and political in origin. However, although it is clear that this conflict would have had a plethora of causes, it is simply not possible to claim that religion had nothing to do with it. At the very least it enabled people to justify to themselves what they were doing, because they were acting in the interests of the true faith which was being threatened by the heretics from the other camp.

The key is to try and identify what it is about religion in particular which engenders these extreme types of behaviour. In this context I think it would be useful to include ideologically driven political beliefs under the same heading, for they share much in common with religious conviction. If you take communism as an example, you have a belief system which claims to be able to dramatically improve human life on Earth. This was also the case with Islam, which was just as much a social and economic revolution as a religious one, and very much included a blueprint for an ideal type of society. Another feature which unites religious

5. RELIGION

and political belief is the violence and suffering which they both entrain. For example, the Russian or Chinese revolutions were both followed by a violence and barbarity, which put into the shade the behaviour of the previous regimes.

What is it about religious or political conviction which engenders such violent reactions when those beliefs are perceived to be threatened? From my perspective it can only mean that they are particularly important in the make-up of our individuality. In the case of religion, by being able to reconcile the fundamental paradoxes which threaten our sense of individuality, i.e. ageing and death, as well as providing both an explanation and a solution for human suffering, we can quickly come to rely on it to make sense of our world. Furthermore, religion obviously relies on the existence of a greater power in the form of God. This notion, upon which all the other facets of religion rest, is in itself hugely relieving to the human beings struggling to deal with all the difficulties that life throws at them. When you add in the fact that many believers think that the only real god is the one they worship, or at least that other religions are not following the true path to God, you can see how people can easily feel threatened even by the mere fact that other people don't have the same conviction as them. If you are a strong believer, your faith is not something that is external to you, but actually forms a part of your makeup. Individuality is, as I have clearly explained, completely artificial, and having no substance of its own, relies on illusory concepts for its existence. Whilst gender, social class and age all play their role along with a host of other concepts, none of them are going to reinforce the existence of the self in the same way as religious belief. Furthermore, religious belief although often inherited, if it is to have any real importance for that person, requires them to attach themselves to it both emotionally and psychologically. A feature of this process is that by having faith, you feel special, in that you develop a relationship with your God. Although a significant part of this process involves talking to God through prayer and devotion, there are many who feel that God speaks to them directly. This theme is very present in the Old Testament of the Bible, where God regularly comes down to Earth in order to directly get his message across to men. The Ten Commandments themselves are an example of this. There are also a number of recent examples where a direct representative of God, such as the Virgin Mary, appears and talks to people. Lourdes, a place which receives thousands of pilgrims a year in search of healing, was created after an apparition by the Virgin Mary and it is only one of many. Once you have created the idea of there being an ultimate power in our world that is incarnated in the form of "God", those who acknowledge his existence will feel special because of their connection to him. They will feel validated and whole because of that belief, and can easily see the fact that other people don't share the same faith as a threat.

Of course, religion does not exist on its own but forms part of an overall cultural and social identity, so that

5. RELIGION

a threat to a person's faith can easily be perceived as a threat to their way of life. When you consider the differences between Islam and Christianity in terms of diet, marriage, gender differences, alcohol, to name but a few, it is easy to understand how these two religions have come to blows. When you add power and money into the mix, the results are pretty predictable. Also, once you have a religion, it is not difficult to manipulate it to serve your interests either cynically or even in apparently good faith. I am sure that many of those persecuting "non-believers" did so in the genuine belief that they were serving God and helping to create a better world. This is where the parallel with politics becomes so obvious. The communist revolutionaries in Russia believed that they were acting in the best interests of the "people" and were thus able to justify the atrocities that many committed. For them the "God" whom they served was no longer the Christian one, but rather the idea of "the will of the people". But both ideas, be it the "will of God" or the "will of the people" are as nebulous and meaningless as each other, and simply serve as a justification for behaviour that is all about shoring up the egos of those involved. In the case of the communist revolutionaries in Russia, it was all about creating a better and fairer world for the people, which meant those pursuing this goal could feel good about themselves even if this meant killing and torturing. After all, it was all in the name of the greater good and if a few reactionaries had to be liquidated in the process then so be it! In effect the world is being divided up into "good" and "evil" forces, and in order for "good" to triumph, the evil forces have to be destroyed. Obviously not all believers, either religious or political, will go to these extremes, but because of the importance these belief systems play in terms of identity and culture, it is possible to understand how it happens.

So, religion is able to give us anchors and a feeling of having significance as an individual. This is very much reflected in the way God has been portrayed over the centuries. As a child I always remember being puzzled by the fact that God was usually depicted as an old man with a beard! For starters why on earth is God masculine? Obviously in the English language you are going to end up having to use the label he or she, and it is pretty obvious why the male pronoun prevailed. However, when you think about it logically there is no reason at all why a God or supreme being would bear any resemblance to us humans at all. Indeed given that such a God is likely to be immortal, all knowing and all seeing, it seems extremely unlikely. However, the reality is that for most believers, God has to be someone whom they can relate to and the most popular view of this God seems to be the one which resembles a father figure. This is because a father figure is someone who cares and looks after you and makes you feel special. He is someone whom you can rely on and who can come to your aid in times of distress. Of course, God could just as easily be (and perhaps it would be more logical) a mother figure; however, because the monotheistic religions were founded and have developed in patriarchal societies, it would have been unthinkable

5. RELIGION

for God to be a woman! God has to make sense in terms of the society we live in, which is why Christianity was not only very different in its early days, but has since split up into a plethora of different churches and groups.

This reality is reflected by the enormous variety of religious beliefs which have existed throughout the ages. Furthermore, as is clear from modern society, people are able to live without any religion at all and it seems very likely that this was the case for many of those that lived before the development of agriculture. Amazingly enough there are some remaining hunter gatherer societies who even today live without religion as we know it. (9) The Hazda who are a small tribe living in Tanzania seem to have not only no religion but not even a notion of an afterlife. Because their world has remained sufficiently connected to their immediate environment, they have simply not had the need to create a religion. They do not have to come up with complicated solutions to resolve the contradiction between our sense of individuality and the unavoidable reality of ageing and death, which puts the realness of our separate existence into question. Yes, they obviously have a sense of being individuals, but the parameters of that world are much smaller than our own. Without a calendar or any spatial coordinates, i.e. measurements for distance, geographical position etc. they are limited to a much smaller artificial space-time world, and as a result are much more part of their environment. They are not able to feel as we do, completely separate to the world.

This separation is reflected in our use of the word "the environment". This term has always puzzled me, because it assumes that we are completely separate to it. You often hear that "environmental concerns" need to be taken into account when deciding on how to implement a particular project or policy, i.e. a new airport, road or factory. This type of approach implicitly includes the supposition that the environment is totally separate to us human beings, but for various reasons (maybe even our survival!) we need to take its needs into account. To a hunter gatherer such as the Hadza, this type of thinking would make no sense because the environment is their world. In short, just as much as any other being, plant or even geographical feature such as a river, they are the environment! For them, our type of religion which is based on a concept of individuality stretching way beyond death, and involving the judgement of all our worldly actions by a Supreme Being or God would quite simply be impossible. If like the Hadza you don't have a concept of days, weeks or years, (they can only count up to three or four) or of space beyond the landmarks which make up your world, there is no way you can begin to imagine yourself being judged for everything you have done in your life by "God". The highly developed space-time matrix in addition to the complex morality which you would require for this would simply not exist. If a member of the Hadza tribe behaved in a manner which was considered unacceptable, the result is likely to be resolution of the problem or their expulsion. The issue would have to be dealt with as it arose, because it would be affecting their lives then and there. To them,

5. RELIGION

the idea of trying someone for something they did 10 years ago by sending them to jail for the next 10 years would be simply incomprehensible. I read recently about another tribe, this time in the Amazon, whose language had absolutely no notion of time in it. (10) The Amondawa, according to researchers from the University of Portsmouth and the Federal University of Rondonia in Brazil, simply refer to meeting in the afternoon or the next day. Just as in the case of the Hadza, they don't have a calendar or notions of years, months or weeks and can only count up to four. The fact that their language does not have these concepts in it, inevitably means that their perception of life will be different. If we take the concept of dying, without having a notion of years the idea of when you are going to die is inevitably much vaguer with the net result that you will worry about it less! The same applies to all the different aspects of our lives, be it having a career, planning a holiday or even catching a train or an aeroplane. As I said at the very start of the book, without a concept of time and space, our society would come to crashing halt, and what is interesting about the Amondawa is that even today there are humans whose language, which I have already indicated is the basis of our shared notion of reality, does not allow them to live as we do. This includes our concept of religion which relies on having a strong enough notion of individuality to imagine life after death. As such it is clear that our notion of religion and God is completely dependent on our constructed view of the world and its associated social structures.

Until about 200 years ago, although there were frequent splits within the Christian faith, it was almost inconceivable for someone to declare that they did not believe in God. However, in 1882 Friedrich Nietzsche in his book "The Gay Science" writes the famous line "God is dead".

Over the last 100 years or more these prophetic words have come to be realised and today in most developed societies, especially in Western Europe, religion has all but disappeared. Bar a few exceptions, the churches are empty, with the bulk of the population happy to have themselves classified as "agnostic" or not knowing. The vast majority of people who are baptised only have it done (or more precisely for most of them, their parents have it done) for largely social reasons. Yes, a lot of people might still get married and buried by a priest, but for most it is because they feel more comfortable with the traditional way of doing things. The reality is that in a northern European country such as the UK, there are probably more practising Muslims, i.e. those who worship on a regular basis, than Christians, even though Muslims make up less than 10% of the population. Religious feasts such as Christmas and Easter have been almost completely stripped of their religious significance and have instead become family holidays, which especially in the case of Christmas are dominated by rampant consumerism. What is extraordinary about this is that on the face of it our sense of individuality is constantly increasing as the parameters of our world expand. Compared to the

5. RELIGION

medieval period where maps were rare and valuable, and most people had no idea of what went on outside their locality, today's situation could not be more different. At a touch of a button using a program such as Google Earth, you can beam in and look at any part of the globe. There are even programs which allow you to look at the inside of the human body! In a sense the world has been divided up ever more minutely and precisely. The result is that our illusory world has become ever more concrete as has our individuality alongside it. Using the internet, you can look at pictures of a place the other side of the world, and then plan and book how to get there. You will know your departure and arrival time, the precise itinerary you will take and more or less the exact conditions you can expect during your journey. Imagine the difference between travelling to Australia 200 years ago and today, the two experiences would have simply nothing in common!

So given that today we are more certain than we have ever been about our existence as individuals, how come we are able to do away with the drug of religion? Are we by some miracle suddenly able to accept our mortality, or is there perhaps something else going on here? To me the most obvious change is that life has become much safer and more predictable. Infant mortality has fallen dramatically, to the point where it is almost unheard of for a mother to lose her baby in childbirth, and once born almost all children make it through to adulthood. If a baby or a child does die, it is a terrible shock because it has become so rare.

Partly because of this change, life expectancy has improved dramatically, with most people expected to live until at least their seventies and many more into their eighties and nineties. The obvious reason for this extraordinary change is simple: science. In the last 200 years, our lives have been transformed by medicine, public health measures and economic prosperity. Clean water, proper sewage systems, food and shelter as well as medical advances such as vaccines and antibiotics have completely altered our lives. We can now keep insulin dependent diabetics alive, do organ transplants, cure leprosy, TB and malaria, as well as myriad other incredible medical and surgical interventions. Indeed, the general perception is that if you have a problem medicine will be able to sort it out and even if nothing can be done, the expectation is that we will be able to cure it in the future. Even the ultimate illness of old age is gradually being challenged. It is said that today's 60 or maybe even 70 year olds are yesterday's 50 year olds. I even heard of a 101 year old man who ran a 26 mile marathon! Today, age is less and less of a barrier to doing almost anything. Until a few years ago, women were simply unable to have children much beyond their mid-40s. Today because of IVF there are women in their 60s who have had babies. This trend has spread into almost every sphere of life, as the example of the 100 year old marathon runner exemplifies. In fact, you hear talk that before too long science will find ways to slow the ageing process right down so that eventually we will be able to live for hundreds of years! The net result of all of this is that we feel much more secure about

5. RELIGION

the permanence of our existence and feel that to some extent at least we are beginning to defeat the twin evils of ageing and death.

All of these changes have happened in the context of the general evolution of science from a very isolated discipline, often treated with suspicion, to the dominant philosophical approach of the modern era. With its origins in the renaissance some 500 years ago, science has gradually expanded and developed itself to the point where it is able to explain almost everything in our world. Today the black death is no longer viewed as being the result of "bad air", God's rage or even the Jews (who were killed in their thousands), but of a bacterium. This is equally applicable to all aspects of our world, whether it is the causes of flooding, fires, or any other natural or manmade disaster. In addition, we have gradually been able to piece together "how things work", and have been able to use this knowledge to harness nature to our ends. This is how we have ended up living in our technological world of the internet, space exploration, high speed rail and all the other myriad technologies which we depend on to live our lives. Furthermore, as I have already mentioned, we live in a civilized bubble, cut off from nature and only in extreme circumstances such as floods and earthquakes, do we remember it is there.

Our general sense is that we now control and dominate our world, and this has reached such a level that we now have to preserve nature from our destructive actions.

Given this situation, it is little wonder that God and religion have begun to take a back seat!

Even the insoluble problem of death has been, if not solved, then at least put out of sight. Does it not seem strange to any of you, that elderly people have mostly been swept from our midst? Until the 1950s it was pretty normal for extended families to live together, and grandparents stayed with their families until they died. This is still very much case in most of the third world, although as they become more westernized, they are gradually adopting the western model. Today in the developed world, a huge proportion of the elderly population lives in retirement homes, where they patiently sit and wait to die, out of sight of their family and the general population. Because of this, most of us simply don't see people get very old and die and as a result death has increasingly disappeared from mainstream society. When you add to this that death either in childhood or in adulthood has also diminished hugely, it becomes clear that even though we may be aware of it at a subconscious level, we are able to cast it aside for most of our daily lives. Not only have the elderly been parked conveniently out of the way, but we have done the same for disabled people or indeed anyone else deemed to be different from "normal". This was not the case a few hundred years ago and is still not in most less developed countries. In Africa I frequently saw people with disabilities both mental and physical living in towns and villages, interacting normally with the rest of the population. In Europe until

5. RELIGION

relatively recently it was considered normal to have a "village madman", yet today anything which gets in the way or puts into doubt the solid foundations and good functioning of our world is simply put out of sight.

From a religious perspective the net result is that having banished ill health, ageing, disability and even dying from our midst, we are also able to banish religion. In its place we have science which can now explain almost everything in our world, as well as constantly improving our security, health and longevity. Obviously there are still plenty of believers, but the more modern consumerist civilisation spreads, the less important religion seems to be. Consumerism and all it represents in terms of fleeting gratification is in a sense a bedfellow of science. Because so many more of us are able to boost our sense of self with the accumulation of material goods, we are able to some extent push away the underlying insecurity we all feel. Inevitably the ultimate result is to make things worse, but that doesn't make the drug any less attractive. Perhaps it is also because as a society we are all much more educated and sophisticated than we were in the medieval period, when only the favoured few could read. As a result, we are no longer prepared to accept the simplistic solutions offered by the traditional churches, and instead feel more comfortable admitting that we don't know.

However, as appealing as it might be, the fact that in many countries religion is declining, does not unfortunately mean that the "human paradox "is disappearing. Unsurprisingly, quite the opposite is true, as despite extraordinary levels of wealth and health compared to even 50 years ago, the rates of depression are soaring. Yes, we might be safer, healthier, richer and live longer, but we don't seem to be any happier. So, although for the various reasons I have outlined, we are turning much less to religion to try and deal with our insecurities, we are inevitably just as far away as ever from managing to live comfortably with our totally unstable and illusory situation. We have simply replaced religion with science and consumerism, and as I have already mentioned, this change has required a completely new level of education. Perhaps this explains why it is generally among the less well educated and more traditional societies that religion still has a strong hold.

6. EDUCATION

Although there might be disagreement about which type of education is most suitable for our children, no one ever seems to question why it is we all need to study for so many years. We simply accept that it is what enables people to get ahead in life and achieve whatever aims they might have. Of course, in a basic way, education of some sort exists in many species. If I come back to my dog, when we first had him at about four months old, he needed a lot of training, in order to make him a socially acceptable pet. The same was true of my children who needed years to learn the basic rules of human behaviour! However, by the time a child goes to school they will generally be toilet trained, know how to feed themselves, be able to speak, walk and run and have all the other basic things needed for functioning as a human being. So why on earth should they need another 12+ years before they are considered educated enough to make their own way in society?

On the face of it the answer is obvious: the human world is much more complex than that of animals and therefore requires a much longer educational process. After all, we have much bigger brains and the requirements needed to function in our societies are more complicated and challenging than for any animals. However, it is also the case that human societies have not always and even today do not always educate their children the way we do in modern societies. So, what is it about our society that demands such a long apprenticeship, with years of study needed to gain even the most basic of skills?

The answer is clearly to be found in a shift from learning about concrete environmental features like the functions of different tools and objects to completely abstract concepts such as places and times. Of course, as I have already described, abstraction is also required to make sense of our immediate environment. An example is that when we learn about trees in general, we are abstracting the idea of tree. However, in this type of process you are able to look at, and touch trees and it is therefore relatively easy to understand. But a purely abstract concept is much more difficult to make sense of. So, if we talk about tomorrow, you are never going to be able to see it or touch it, meaning you can't just point at it and give it a name. The same is true for all completely abstract ideas, whether it be days of the week, months, and concepts such as freedom or poverty or even geographical notions such as countries or cities. In order for people to be able to fully understand these ideas, you first need to create a framework in which

6. EDUCATION

these concepts make sense. For young children, up to about eight or nine years old, it is very difficult for them to grasp these abstractions. My children used to get terribly confused about the idea of London being in England. For them London was the world they lived in and what that had to do with England was quite beyond them. Indeed, the only kind of geographical locations which made sense were places they had been to and these were only understood in terms of their own memories. So, for example, "Corsica" was the villa where we spent our summer holidays. If a child has no reference point at all for a concept, it will be almost impossible for them to make any sense of it. As a result, an idea such as freedom or individual rights will take much longer to make any sense, and children are unlikely to study it until quite late on in their education. However, what all these abstract concepts rely on is an understanding of space-time. In the case of yesterday and tomorrow this is perfectly obvious, but it is also the case for all the other abstract concepts which make up our world.

It is therefore no surprise that the first two subjects which are studied at school and are considered the basis of any education are literacy and numeracy, or language and numbers. This is where we all start and if we fail to grasp them we have little hope of learning much else. Language, which includes the use of numbers, is the cement which glues together our illusory world and is what enables us to function as though all the abstract concepts we habitually rely on really exist. This in turn is totally dependent on the structure of our space-time world even if we are not at all aware of it. The first things that children learn at school are how to recognise letters and numbers, and then basic words. This is in a sense the first step in the transition from the solid touchable world to the one which exists solely in our heads. At the beginning when they are learning numbers it is easy to represent a number by holding up some fingers or using pencils. A low number, say up to 10, is easily represented in this way and this allows us to provide the basis upon which numeracy can be built on. The same is true with letters and words. You can start by pointing letters out, which if necessary can be touched as well as seen. It is then possible to ascribe sounds to them. Once you have acquired this knowledge, you can start to make basic words which will represent definite objects. Of course, most children will come to primary school with at least the spoken aspect of language and a basic understanding of numbers. What school is doing is adding the written aspect to this which will then enable them to go much further.

If we take mathematics, as long as your knowledge of numbers remains unwritten, you are going to find it much more difficult to learn arithmetic and will never be able to acquire the skills to use mathematics for anything but the most basic tasks. Without a mastery of written numbers, how are you going to be able to imagine numbers that you can't count? For example, the figure of a million is likely to be meaningless unless you are able to write it down. The same is true for language,

6. EDUCATION

where an inability to read or write and to understand the finer points of language is going to hugely limit your ability to understand and communicate with others. Formal education, therefore, is the bridge which enables you to fully join the immensely complex and very fluid world we live in today.

Once you have mastered the basics of reading and writing letters and numbers, the process is able to start moving up a gear. It is now that truly abstract ideas can start to be presented and made sense of. In the case of language, you start to leave simple descriptive sentences such as "the cat is on the mat" and instead explore abstract concepts such as the "the cat sat on the mat". This is where the structure of language becomes so important in creating our world, because it is putting forward ideas of situations that don't actually exist. It is quite a leap of imagination for a young child to accept that something happened in the past and that it is no longer the case now. I have already mentioned how through learning Italian and listening to my children's experiences of learning grammar, I realised the difficulty and importance of learning the various tenses which our use of language is based on. For example, for the past you can say: I have eaten, I have been eating, I wanted to have eaten, I should have eaten, I might have eaten etc. When you begin to really look at it, the potential permutations really are endless and they reflect the way we live our lives. In order to be able to properly understand what others are saying and then communicate yourself, you need to have fully mastered all these concepts. Once you have done so, and it becomes automatic, you can interact fully with human society. When you add in a grasp of numbers and mathematics, you can quantify the concepts that have been created by language. One of the principal mechanisms, which enable this process, is learning to tell the time, which you are only going to be able to do once you have a good grasp of numbers. This then allows you to quantify the various ideas of future and past which you are learning in grammar. Indeed, one of the most important aspects of school is timekeeping, i.e. learning to live by the clock, and this can be a real challenge for children. Yet if you are going to be able to live and work in the modern world, it is absolutely essential. Learning the structures of grammar and time is very much part of the same process and together allow children access to the adult world.

It is then that subjects such as history, geography and science start being taught. Children now that they have the tools with which to make sense of things can start to become fully immersed in our culture. This process is not, of course, an isolated one but happens alongside the gradual building up of a child's identity. So, whilst they learn about geography, they will obviously be becoming aware of which country they belong to or live in and what the attributes of that country are. How large it is, where it is situated in the world, its climate, topography and language. At the same time, they will be gradually assimilating the fact that they have a particular nationality and that some others don't have

6. EDUCATION

it. My teenage son is acutely aware of nationality and the supposed attributes of different countries. History obviously plays a major role in this as it gives a sense of context, by providing the background of how a particular nation got to where it is today. None of this is random but is a carefully developed programme to give children a sense of individual and collective identity, as well as an ability to share the concepts of the adult world. In this way a huge artificial world is gradually revealed to children with the framework of space-time as the foundation. The explanation for how this world works is provided by science, which seeks to unravel the mechanics of our universe. So not only are we able to explain that something works in a particular way, e.g. that it snows in winter, but also why. This, of course, is a hugely powerful tool because children are not only taught what our world is made up of, but also how it works. For example, we know that we breathe in oxygen and breathe out carbon dioxide and that this is mediated by the lungs and the blood. This type of information, which explains the functioning of so many events, systems and living organisms, makes our shared world indisputably real. Furthermore, it introduces children to the idea that we are actually able to manipulate our environment because it is separate to us. They are gradually taught how adults view and use the world, i.e. that this environment can be divided up, categorised and understood. This process is based on two principles, the creation of our own individuality separated from everything else, and the dividing up and categorisation of everything that is not us. However, we do not only categorise our immediate environment, but also the artificial world of shared concepts. This artificial world is in itself based on separation and categorisation, and because of its enormous and ever growing scope, it requires endlessly more learning to be made sense of.

The more educated someone becomes, the further away they are likely to get from feeling part of their environment. This is perhaps why we have a caricature of mad professors as people who are totally unaware of what is going on around them. In the developed world everyone receives an education until at least 16, meaning that almost everybody spends at least 10 years in formal education. In Europe over the last 100 years we have changed from a situation in which relatively few people received a good education, with numeracy and literacy much lower than today, to almost completely literate populations. This has gradually transformed our society into the knowledge-based world we live in. As a result, the world of knowledge has become ever more complex and large, which is why increasing numbers of people continue their education way past 16. In the UK there has been an explosion in the number of universities, and recent governments have made it a policy to try and get as many young people as possible to go. At the same time, technology and social trends have united to create new forms of communication mediated through the internet such as social networking, blogging etc. It is now possible to have a community of friends or professional colleagues

6. EDUCATION

who are spread around the globe but are in constant real time communication with each other. To those who use them, these systems seem completely normal; however, it requires a great deal of sophistication and education to do so. Yet the development required to get to this stage is not at all obvious because all those participating are more or less at the same level. It is a little like the programming which underlies computer software, i.e. totally hidden from the users. Of course, there is nothing stopping anyone from looking into the programming, it is just that 99% of people are only interested in using it and not what makes it work.

As a child I always wondered how on earth we had accumulated enough knowledge for our world to function, e.g. how had we worked out how to send rockets to the moon? It would obviously not have been possible for a cave man to have worked it out from scratch! The answer clearly lies in the educational process, which not only enables people to understand and participate in the world, but also to develop it further and then pass it on to the next generation. Whilst a basic education gives you the essential tools for understanding and participating in society, further education enables you to build and develop society further. In a sense education is the dynamic which expands and complexifies our illusory world ever further. At the cutting edge of this process, whether it is in the field of science, technology or business, education becomes research and design. The discoveries, inventions and creations which result from this then become part of our world and are later taught to school children and university students. This is why the educational process is becoming longer and longer. It is a societal process in which the individual acts as part of a larger organism. Yes, specific people such as Einstein might well have greatly expanded the field of human knowledge, but this could not have been the case without all the learning and discoveries which had taken place before. The same is true for all new human theories and inventions.

So, we have a gradually expanding world of knowledge, which requires ever more complex ideas and theories to function. Whilst most of us are able to grasp Newtonian physics fairly easily, many of us would struggle to make sense of Einstein. However, when it comes to today's theories, whether it be in astro-physics or quantum mechanics, the average person has almost no chance of understanding anything at all. I have recently heard scientists talking about how there may be more than four dimensions, perhaps as many as six or seven. I can't even begin to make any sense of this and can only imagine that highly complex mathematical formulas lie behind this idea. The level of education required to even be able to have the vaguest notion of what is being talked about is obviously very high.

What is going on is an endless process of increasing complexity and specialisation which, because it is based on an illusory notion of space and time, requires the building up of our shared reality. Even though the obvious symptoms of this dynamic are technological

6. EDUCATION

and professional, it actually affects every single aspect of our lives. So, if you take simple activities such as getting from A to B, whereas a couple of hundred years ago you would just get up and walk there, today you need to know how to use public transport or drive a car. You might also need to know how to use a GPS system or a computer in order to book your train or aeroplane. For those who don't keep up with these changes, life can become very difficult. For example, it is almost impossible to book an aeroplane ticket without knowing how to use the internet. Those who can't, either rely on others or simply don't travel by air.

This situation affects almost every aspect of life, whether it is shopping, cooking, social relationships or even completely natural events such as giving birth. Today in advanced economies women all go through birth preparation classes in which they are taught what to expect, what painkillers and procedures are available to help them and what they can do to be prepared. Obviously, you can still give birth without any of this, but it would be very bewildering to suddenly find yourself in a medicalised birth situation if you don't have a clue what is going on! However, attending birth preparation classes without first having studied some human biology, which in turn requires literacy and numeracy, would be totally pointless. You can't put a current day hunter gatherer such as the Hadza in a birth preparation class and expect her to understand anything at all!

When you begin to understand how absolutely vast, complex and changeable our reality is, it is easy to understand the vital role that education plays. With globalisation mediated through structures such as the internet, this is becoming ever truer. When people lived in small, isolated communities, the parameters of their world were much smaller and consequently so was their need for education. For hunter gatherer groups such as the Hadza, there is simply no need for formal education. All necessary knowledge including language is directly taught to children by the adults of the community. They would definitely have a much deeper and greater knowledge of their immediate environment, i.e. animals, plants etc., but because they are free of our vast illusory reality, their overall need for knowledge is much reduced. This was the case for the vast majority of the world's population until only recently. However, there is of course a major difference between the lack of education in hunter gatherer society and the situation in pre-renaissance Europe. In the case of hunter gatherers, it was the case for all of society, whilst for medieval European society, the elite were relatively well educated. Education not only gave access to a world of knowledge but also to power. The majority who were denied education would have found changing their social situation almost impossible partly because they didn't have the necessary tools. If you are innumerate and illiterate, your world is going to be much smaller and it is going to be much easier to control you. You would have no access to most accumulated knowledge which would have been found in books and you would

6. EDUCATION

therefore be much likelier to defer to those who did. This must have made it much easier for institutions such as the medieval church to control their believers. If your religion is based on the written word, and you have no access to this (books were also closely guarded) you are much more likely to defer to those who do. This is perhaps one of the reasons that protestant churches, such as the Lutherans, believed in a direct relationship with God, which did not require the mediation of a priest. It is perhaps not particularly surprising that this change happened at around the same time that knowledge was being demystified by the development of printing.

Education continues even today to be used as a tool of control, with groups such as the Taliban in Afghanistan attempting to prevent the education of women. I can only imagine that those who wish to stop women being educated believe that it would in some way undermine their social structures. By having the wider world revealed to them, they would become empowered and as a result would want to change their situation and thus society as a whole. Other societies have taken a rather different approach and have developed education specifically to reinforce their political structures. The classic example is the old Soviet Union where one of the purposes of education was to lead people to believe in the system and of course see different societies, specifically the capitalist societies of the West, as both a threat and dysfunctional. Ironically, the West and the US in particular did exactly the same thing, with the

Soviet Union routinely seen as a threat to freedom and hell bent on destroying us.

This aspect of education reaches its extremes in notions such as re-education, which has been and may still be used by regimes to bring wayward citizens back into line. The idea is to realign that person's perception of reality with the political vision of the regime. This type of education is also known as brain washing and is reported as being used not only by regimes but also religious sects. I always remember being told about people becoming part of sects such as the Moonies, where they were brainwashed into believing their doctrine. The norms of behaviour which wider modern society sees as acceptable have simply been replaced by another approach which is quickly seen as a threat to the conventional way of life. Just as in the case of the Soviet Union and the West in the Cold War, education is the process by which identity is built up. Of course, identity is a very fragile construct, and this is the reason that people find it so much easier to attach themselves to strong belief systems. However, to even get to the stage where you are going to be able to understand the beliefs of a sect like the Moonies, you need to be educated enough for their concepts to make sense to you.

Education is therefore a multifaceted process as it allows people access to our shared illusory world and at the same time creates their identity within it. This is why one's education in the wider sense is such an important

6. EDUCATION

factor in how we perceive ourselves and others. In fact, you can only have access to human society if you are part of it and this requires you to perceive yourself in the same way as most other people. If you have none of the basic concepts required to engage with other humans on their terms, all you will be aware of is the immediate environment you find yourself in. The idea of here and there, yesterday and tomorrow, and even individual existence would not exist. This is the state that those who practise meditation, are actually seeking to get into, i.e. a complete emptying of the mind. If you are completely free of these concepts you are also going to be free of everything that accompanies them such as worrying about your future. So, education, although it can be considered to liberate us from our position in society and from the power of others, is also what embeds us in society. It is what allows us to understand and use our space-time framework, via the mechanisms of language and numbers, to construct our sense of self. It is what gradually convinces us of the reality of our world and consequently bit by bit squeezes an immediate childlike awareness out of us. Of course, this could not happen if we were not genetically predisposed for this process, and so is probably an inevitable part of human development. Although I am definitely not suggesting scrapping all education as the way to eradicate human suffering, this does not stop it being the principal mechanism enabling us to believe in our independent existences.

Although there is no solution to this situation, it is at least helpful to understand where we are rather than blindly accepting things as they are. At the beginning of this chapter I spoke about how education is universally seen as a good thing, and it is clear that in terms of advancing one's position and giving ourselves more choices it is the case. However, I don't see any evidence that it has made humanity any happier. I will never forget a journey I made from Cameroon in Africa back to the UK some 20 years ago. The Africa we had left was a thousand times more alive than home and it made me realise that wealth and education are perhaps not the great panacea we believe them to be. Yes, most African people might generally be less educated, yet I can't see any evidence that it is detrimental to their well-being. This is clearly supported by studies which show that it is in developed, highly educated countries such as France where people suffer most from depression and anxiety. An incredibly high proportion of the population takes anti-depressants and people are generally anxious and apprehensive about the future.

(12) In fact, according to recent research into rates of depression in 18 countries, it is more likely to strike in high-income countries than in poor ones. The most depressed country of all was France with a rate of 21% of the population, and the US followed close behind with 19.2%. The study, undertaken by the World Health Organization and published in the journal BMC Medicine, found that the average lifetime prevalence of major depression in the 10 high-income countries

6. EDUCATION

in the study was 14.6 per cent. In the eight low- and middle-income countries, the lifetime prevalence of major depression was 11.1 per cent. So it seems that depression can be regarded as a disease of education and affluence.

At first glance this seems completely nonsensical and tends to baffle economists who almost all work on the premise that economic development is beneficial. Even if today more people are questioning whether getting endlessly richer actually achieves anything, almost no one questions the benefit of education itself.

In fact, there is a strong current of thought which is convinced that by gradually becoming more educated the world will become a better place. We will become more informed and behave in a more rational fashion. Yet what evidence is there that this is the case? The horrors of the first and second world wars were not committed in some far-off underdeveloped land but in Europe, the most educated, richest and civilised continent on Earth! Being highly educated is obviously no bar to behaving badly and as the case of France shows, it is quite probable that an educated population is less content and more worried than an uneducated one. When you think about it, it is both obvious and logical that this might be the case. If because of your education you live almost completely in an illusory reality, which by its nature causes you to suffer, you are hardly likely to be relaxed and happy! If you spend your life believing that you are truly an individual and struggle against ageing, the coming of death, and all the other threats to your individual existence, life is likely to be a stressful experience.

Education is particularly interesting because unlike money, religion and even morality it does not have any potential negative connotations. It is instead associated with outcomes which our society regards as positive such as more individual freedom, better career prospects, more civilised behaviour, and most of the other features which we associate with free, modern democratic societies. There is a widespread belief that as societies become richer and better educated, they will move towards a fairer and more democratic type of society. We often talk about the fact that less developed countries need to go through the same stages of development as the rich ones, in order to become fairer and freer. This view might be disputed by the leaders of totalitarian countries such as China, as they are likely to find the job of ruling a country of increasingly educated and informed people ever more difficult. This is why they try to censor the internet and the media.

This process demonstrates the close link between education and individuality. Perhaps it is no surprise that in any kind of dictatorship the first group of people to be rounded up are the intellectuals, whose education and individuality is seen as a threat to the regime. In the case of the rich liberal democracies, which embrace individuality and freedom of choice, the opposite is true. Education is seen as an essential

6. EDUCATION

human right along with freedom of speech and all the other personal freedoms we enjoy. For this reason, the high rates of unhappiness in rich countries must be very baffling to those who believe freedom and democracy are signs of human progress. However, this apparently paradoxical situation only exists because we believe that our individuality is real, and that freedom is about guaranteeing the preservation of what we believe makes us truly individual.

7. FREEDOM OR STOP MAKING SENSE

It might seem from what I have written so far that the human condition is a totally desperate one, based as it is on an illusory notion of individuality. If this were not bad enough, the various attempts, we make to shore it up through the mechanisms of property, morality, religion, technology and any anything else we can dream up only make matters infinitely worse. Furthermore, despite a widespread belief in progress, we are in reality making no headway at all in changing our situation. If anything, the path humanity is on seems to make our apparent individuality more, not less, real, increasing the potential for suffering and pain. It really would be difficult for me to paint a bleaker picture, particularly in light of the fact that it all seems to be inevitable. Whatever aspect of the human condition you examine, be it morality, money or religion, all seem to be the natural response to the challenge of convincing ourselves that we are solid, permanent and important

7. FREEDOM OR STOP MAKING SENSE

despite overwhelming evidence to the contrary. This is perfectly summed up in the classical notion of "freedom" which only makes sense in the context of individuality. We generally believe that through being free we have choice, and that this choice will enable us to be fulfilled as human beings. Yet it is obvious that this idea of freedom is totally illusory as the individual simply doesn't exist in the way we suppose.

So, are we simply doomed to suffer in our illusory world, or is there perhaps another path which can verily liberate us from the endless cycle of anxiety and insecurity we live in? If so, this approach can have absolutely nothing to do with us as individuals or the space-time matrix it is based on. Perhaps the first and most important step is instead of endlessly trying to make sense of our world, to try and observe our surroundings in a completely passive way. This requires no effort, judgement or belief, but rather a "choiceless awareness". It involves a shift from interacting with our reality with purpose to a perception that involves no belief or desire. By stopping trying to make sense we accept that there is no "real reality" which we can all hang onto, and consequently there is no need to keep struggling and striving to feel secure. There has been life on earth for millions of years and the very fact that we exist is testament to the wonder of life. We as humans have had nothing to do with that process and it will continue regardless of what we do. However, we are able to choose whether or not to reconnect to the world around us.

Today even science, the great religion of rationality, has begun to see the limits of the idea of reality. Newton by discovering gravity up-ended our instinctive ideas about weight or an absolute up and down. We may accept the idea of gravity without questioning but we still live our daily lives as though Newton had never made the breakthrough. The same is true with regard to time, which we continue to see as unfolding in a regular and unchanging manner, in a direct contradiction to Einstein's General Theory of Relativity where time is described as an elastic phenomenon. Even more difficult to imagine is quantum mechanics' assertion that nothing exists unless it is being observed! In short, science, rather than reinforcing our natural perspective on reality, has actually pulled the rug from beneath our feet, refuting the reality that makes sense to us and that we depend on for our daily lives. Even more bizarrely, different currents in science, e.g. Einsteinian relativity and quantum mechanics, appear to contradict each other. Perhaps we just need to accept that there is no one "objective reality" but different scenarios that work in a specific set of circumstances. No being's perception is ever identical, whether you are talking about dogs, dolphins or humans, and no one reality can be described as any more valid than any other. Oddly enough many of the most amazing things in life, whether it be a mother's love, incredible music, or a beautiful view, are essentially unexplainable. To try to make sense of everything is a pointless reductionist process that leads nowhere except to bigotry and failure. It makes people feel important, able to give

7. FREEDOM OR STOP MAKING SENSE

themselves impressive titles and pontificate to other less well qualified beings. But it in no way enables us to understand and, much more importantly, enjoy life. Almost all the suffering we endure is a result of our feeble attempts to makes sense and control our world. This is what leads to environmental catastrophe, war, torture, stress, conflict and all the other sufferings that torment the human race.

In this book I have aimed to show the reader that all of our beliefs and certainties are illusory and pointless. The inevitable consequence is that it is only by renouncing them that it is possible to be really alive. Does this make me a nihilist or someone who believes in nothing? From a purely semantic perspective perhaps, but only because what I am revealing is undefinable, indescribable, and uncategorizable. Does this mean it doesn't exist? Only in as much as anything, including you or me exists or doesn't exist. Ultimately these are just words, abstractions, approximations that can never capture the infinitely complex, subtle and shifting reality of our perceptual experience. Language, numbers and any other system we have concocted to enable us to communicate and control our environment serve an extremely useful purpose in enabling us to communicate, survive and prosper, but are in no way true representations of our world. Yet we use these systems as though they were reality themselves and base our worlds on them. When Cervantes described Don Quixote as mistaking windmills for knights in armour, he was describing what we all do on a daily basis. We mistake mirages for reality, and are prepared to pillage, destroy and lay waste for them. We may put so called mad people in asylums and stuff them with drugs but who are we kidding? Perhaps those so-called mad people are the only sane ones and are put away because they threaten to reveal the lunacy of rationality? At the very least they are locked up either physically or chemically because they won't or can't buy in to the fantasy that everyone else so happily signs up to.

Virtually all attempts to solve our situation are conceived from within the problem and rather unsurprisingly completely fail to change anything. As the Zen Buddhist saying goes: "the sword cannot cut itself". The problem is our belief in a reality that doesn't exist. It is hardly surprising then, that all attempts to "improve" our reality are doomed to failure. You can't turn a bad mirage into a good one – the only appropriate response is to recognise a mirage for what it is, an optical illusion that doesn't exist. The fact that your brain is convinced, doesn't change anything at all, other than making your life more difficult. It's no good saying, "that type of mirage is a fake but that one over there is real!", yet that is what happens all the time. Whether it's one current of a religion attacking another, scientific rationalists attacking religion, or conventional doctors attacking alternative health practitioners, one belief system is being challenged by another. As I have already explained, even causality, the bedrock of western rationalism, is only one way of looking at things. It may well be that it is what has enabled us to

7. FREEDOM OR STOP MAKING SENSE

send a probe to Mars, but I am afraid that doesn't make it any better at deciphering the nature of reality than the hallucinations of someone on LSD. As Heraclitus the Greek philosopher pointed out some 3000 years ago, we humans only have a partial or species-specific view of reality. That it is paradoxical is completely predictable, and an inherent part of our particular situation. We are not gods, and the fact that as Friedrich Nietzsche has so clearly put it, we have ourselves killed God, does not elevate us to that status. Although we might be, as he has also so succinctly put it, clever animals, that doesn't mean we are able to see beyond our situation. In this book all I have tried to do is expose the clever stage scenery that we have built and called reality for what it is: plywood and paint and not the real thing. Whilst watching a play it's essential that you believe what is being performed enough to enjoy the performance, but it would become a problem if you mistook it for reality. In the same way, it is very useful for us to be able to communicate successfully with our fellow humans and to share a common-enough view of reality to interact socially and thrive in our environment. However, if we mistake the symbols we have created to represent our world, with reality, we fall into the trap of believing in mirages. The ancient peoples seemed to have been more able to combine a strong sense of connection to their environment with an ability to plan and communicate with fellow humans. They lived much more closely in harmony with the natural world and were therefore unable to separate themselves off in the way we do. The problem for us is that whilst materially we are perfectly able to live very cut off from nature, psychologically and in almost every other way it is a catastrophe.

Whilst we always have the option of totally rejecting modern life and going back to live in the wild, this is a very impractical option that for most of us would lead to a quick death. Heraclitus tried this solution to escape the refusal of his fellow citizens of Ephesus, to listen to him. He sadly ended up dying in a dung heap trying to cure himself of the dropsy contracted whilst living off the land, where it is said he was then devoured by dogs. Many others have opted for retreating to caves and relying on alms from local people, or choosing to join a monastery or religious orders. In doing so they hope to cut themselves off sufficiently from human civilization to reconnect with their god, nature or whatever it is they feel is missing from their lives. Great traditions such as Zen Buddhism, Sufism, Taoism, as well as multiple other spiritual disciplines have all flowered to help enable us to find our way back. The Buddhist idea of enlightenment is perhaps the most stunning example of this, wherein the enlightened one is fully liberated from the illusion of individuality and the wheel of life. All of these approaches share the aim of liberation from suffering through losing oneself in God, nature, a higher consciousness or whatever anyone chooses to call it.

I think that this fundamental drive is wonderfully summed up by (13) the Mexican poet, Octavio Paz's 1990 Nobel Literature Prize Lecture, "In search of the present" which I was privileged enough to attend.

7. FREEDOM OR STOP MAKING SENSE

"This consciousness of being separate is a constant feature of our spiritual history. It is born at the very moment of our birth: as we are wrenched from the Whole we fall into an alien land. This experience becomes a wound that never heals. It is the unfathomable depth of every man. All our ventures and exploits, all our acts and dreams, are bridges designed to overcome the separation and reunite us with the world and our fellow-beings. Each man's life and the collective history of mankind can thus be seen as attempts to reconstruct the original situation. An unfinished and endless cure for our divided condition. The feeling of separation is bound up with the oldest and vaguest of my memories: the first cry, the first scare. Like every child I built emotional bridges in the imagination to link me to the world and to other people.

"Time was elastic; space was a spinning wheel. All time, past or future, real or imaginary, was pure presence. Space transformed itself ceaselessly. The beyond was here, all was here: a valley, a mountain, a distant country, the neighbour's patio.

"When was the spell broken? Gradually rather than suddenly, from that moment time began to fracture more and more. And there was a plurality of spaces.

"I accepted the inevitable: I became an adult. That was how my expulsion from the present began. It may seem paradoxical to say that we have been expelled from the present, but it is a feeling we have all had at some moment. Some of us experienced it first as a condemnation, later transformed into consciousness and action. The search for the present is neither the pursuit of an earthly paradise nor that of a timeless eternity: it is the search for a real reality."

Yet despite thousands of years of spiritual practice it appears that humanity only seems to become more convinced of the truth of its rationality. Poets, writers, spiritual teachers may all show us the cracks in the walls that imprison us, but we endlessly ignore them whilst continuing to believe in fairy tales. We chase our tails around and around, convinced that, somehow, we are on the right path and that we will find solutions to all our problems. Medical advances will solve all our health problems, technology will cure the world of environmental catastrophe, democracy and liberalism will rid us of poverty and discrimination, and we will all find ourselves in a Shangri-La of freedom and happiness. All our problems are blamed on others, be it evil corporations, dictators, macho men, extremists of whatever hue, religions, and any other group, however nebulous, that is perceived as an exploiter or manipulator. From time to time an attempt is made to rid society of these corrupt and destructive influences with predictable consequences, usually the deaths of millions of people accompanied by unimaginable suffering.

Yet what is always lacking is the discernment to see the trap of individuality and all its consequences, rather than clinging to the conviction that we are able to change ourselves or anyone else for the better. This will only lead to disappointment, pain and very often

7. FREEDOM OR STOP MAKING SENSE

violence. The potential impacts are endlessly varied, which is why fields such as psychology will always struggle to make any sense of our behaviour.

We need to fundamentally understand that the only real freedom is not based on choice, but rather on liberation from our individuality. This is the only way that we can break free from the yoke of hope, fear, ageing, death and all the other symptoms of our insecurity. Once we know on a fundamental level that we have nothing to lose because we don't actually exist in the way we imagine, we can begin to experience life in a totally different way. Such a direct experience of life has nothing to do with our normal reality, but is in fact pure awareness free from all the worries and concerns we are habitually plagued by. Yet this understanding can only come when we are able to see our situation as it is, when we can see through all the assumptions we base our lives on and become part of the movement of life itself. It is not something which we can achieve or train for, and there is no process or path which can lead us there. All we actually need to do is use our senses to see, smell, hear and feel without any preconceptions or goals.

If we are able to do this then everything becomes easy as all the fears, goals and hopes which depend on our individuality to make sense disappear. However, if we follow the classical path of spiritual development, which is based on an idea of changing and improving our situation we simply replace one set of fears and hopes with another. The problem itself, our belief in our individual existence, remains and is simply repackaged. This is why it is not possible to improve the self, and it is therefore unsurprising that those that try to do this end up disappointed and unhappy.

We are perhaps the only living organisms in the universe who have the capacity to transcend our reality, perhaps with suffering and pain as the necessary corollary to this. Because life expresses itself through the existence of individual organisms there is at the very origin of life a tension between the whole and the part. This can be seen in embryology where the entire process is directed towards complexity and specialisation with the same theme underlying the development of life on earth in general. Yet for all other life forms bar human beings, this paradox does not exist because they are not aware of their own separation. This awareness of being separate, based as it is on an illusory space-time matrix, is both the cause of our pain and at the same time the reason we can transcend our reality. We can have a freedom which is not based on circumstance, but on a realisation that all our problems exist solely in our minds and this has only come about because of our awareness. This does not appear to be the case for other living beings whose happiness is completely dependent on the situation they find themselves in. In this sense we humans are hugely privileged even though we are generally completely unaware of this. Yes, our separation is the cause of our suffering, but it is also what has given us the capacity to directly perceive the movement of life as an unbroken whole.

7. FREEDOM OR STOP MAKING SENSE

So how does this situation actually manifest itself in our daily lives? How do we search for the present? It can obviously have absolutely nothing to do with the artificial space-time world which I have been describing in this book. Furthermore, however strong our belief that the artificial world we all inhabit is actually real, it is absolutely impossible for us not to feel that there is something missing, something that is not quite right. As I have already explained the fundamental obstacle to our freedom is the erroneous belief that we exist as separate beings. Ironically the more caught up we are in our artificial world, and the more we become anchored in our constructed individuality, the less alive we feel. It is as though there is a peculiar trade-off between existing as a separate being and actually experiencing being alive. In a sense this is perfectly obvious as real life is dynamic and in a constant state of change. Trying to capture it or pin it down is like trying to put a river in a container. As in the case of a river, without movement life makes no sense at all. The question then is: how can we rejoin the flow of the river? How in the midst of so many walls and barriers can we be free even for just a moment? Once again, the answer can be found in the difference between humans and other animals. Because other living beings do not have the concept of being separate, they are automatically part and parcel of the movement of life. For them whatever situation they are in, life is just life. Of course, they can suffer, particularly at the hand of humans, but they don't seem to make themselves unhappy. Yes, they have characters and emotions just like we do, but all of that exists within the context of their immediate existence. We, on the other hand, spend almost all of our lives, living in relation to that which is not, i.e. our artificial space-time world, and as I have already explained before, we suffer because of what we imagine having done or experienced, and what we think we might do or experience.

When you think about it, given that we are completely conditioned by both our genes and our upbringing to believe in our existence as individuals and that we think and behave almost 100% along those lines, it is hardly surprising that to deliberately make an effort to rid ourselves of it is so difficult. Even though what you may be trying to do makes sense from an intellectual perspective, how do you actually manage to move from a state of doing to non-doing? How do you take intention out of a process? I spent some time in a meditation centre in Sri Lanka, and came up against this problem directly. The centre was Buddhist and used meditation as its main tool. There are of course myriad meditational traditions and this particular spiritual teacher used mostly guided meditation. Furthermore, in his talks he described the various different steps (based on the Buddhist tradition) which one would have to go through on this spiritual journey. What struck me most, was that the process which people were engaging in was itself rooted in the illusory space-time world. They felt they were on a path in which they were gradually becoming more spiritually liberated and aware. However, the basis of this belief was of course their existence as individuals, since without this idea the process

7. FREEDOM OR STOP MAKING SENSE

made no sense at all. This is in a sense the ultimate paradox, as the ego is trying to liberate itself using the same process by which it is created. This was clearly illustrated by students describing in great detail the different steps they had been through and where they had got to during their meditation. As a result, the path which people believed would liberate them was in fact simply being used as a crutch to convince themselves of their own worthiness. Yes, they may have felt better from following it, but it was never going to be able to liberate them from themselves. This is the principal point which Krishnamurti spent his life making, and wonderfully summed up in his core teaching, contained in the statement made in 1929:

"'Truth is a pathless land'. Man cannot come to it through any organization, through any creed, through any dogma, priest or ritual, not through any philosophic knowledge or psychological technique. He has to find it through the mirror of relationship, through the understanding of the contents of his own mind, through observation and not through intellectual analysis or introspective dissection. Man has built in himself images as a fence of security - religious, political, personal. These manifest as symbols, ideas, beliefs. The burden of these images dominates man's thinking, his relationships and his daily life. These images are the causes of our problems for they divide man from man. His perception of

life is shaped by the concepts already established in his mind.

The content of his consciousness is his entire existence. This content is common to all humanity. The individuality is the name, the form and superficial culture he acquires from tradition and environment. The uniqueness of man does not lie in the superficial but in complete freedom from the content of his consciousness, which is common to all mankind. So he is not an individual.

Freedom is not a reaction; freedom is not a choice. It is man's pretence that because he has choice he is free. Freedom is pure observation without direction, without fear of punishment and reward. Freedom is without motive; freedom is not at the end of the evolution of man but lies in the first step of his existence. In observation one begins to discover the lack of freedom. Freedom is found in the choiceless awareness of our daily existence and activity. Thought is time. Thought is born of experience and knowledge which are inseparable from time and the past. Time is the psychological enemy of man. Our action is based on knowledge and therefore time, so man is always a slave to the past. Thought is ever-limited and so we live in constant conflict and struggle. There is no psychological evolution.

When man becomes aware of the movement of his own thoughts he will see the division between the thinker and thought, the observer

7. FREEDOM OR STOP MAKING SENSE

and the observed, the experiencer and the experience. He will discover that this division is an illusion. Then only is there pure observation which is insight without any shadow of the past or of time. This timeless insight brings about a deep radical mutation in the mind.

Total negation is the essence of the positive. When there is negation of all those things that thought has brought about psychologically, only then is there love, which is compassion and intelligence."

So how then is it possible to make this leap, if there are no paths or techniques which can help us get there? The answer, as so eloquently pointed out by Krishnamurti, is that there is no path or way, simply awareness. You are either living in the real reality or not, and there is no middle ground. It is not something that can be known or rediscovered at will, because it is beyond all learning and knowledge. The reason I have spent so long trying to unravel our artificial world and demonstrate its illusory nature is to enable one to see through it, so that reality can begin to be felt. By becoming aware of what we really are or are not as individuals, we can simply let go and experience life directly. Yet it is clear that very few people are cut out for this approach, which is why the vast majority of those who embark on a spiritual path, end up being trapped in the way I have described. However, the difficulty of transcending individuality doesn't alter the fact that everyone has the need to reconnect with the whole.

We all seek to be taken out of ourselves and to leave our worries behind. This theme is very much to be found in religious and spiritual rituals, where the needs/desires/beliefs of the individual become subsumed in the process. This is what is happening in born again Christian services where people start speaking in tongues and being "taken over by the spirit". They feel that they are no longer in control and are able to let go of their individuality. In this case, their belief is that they are being taken over by "God", which allows them to validate what might otherwise be a frightening process. Although it might seem that this type of behaviour would be restricted to religious and spiritual traditions, this is not at all the case. An obvious example is a football match where the individual identities of the fans can disappear into a shared passion for the side you support. In a good match with the right atmosphere, you literally become part of the crowd, which has a common identity. Your individuality hasn't completely disappeared, but has become part of a larger entity. Another excellent example of this is nationalism, which I have already explained is based on a totally constructed idea, i.e. the nation. Once again it is because people are able to subsume their identity in a greater one and leave aside at least for a while all the suffering and pain associated with maintaining their individual identity. In doing this people are able at least temporarily to feel more alive. The football crowd is totally subsumed by the moment, whether it is in the ecstasy of their team winning a goal and even a match, or the sadness felt if they lose. As a result, you can suddenly feel truly

7. FREEDOM OR STOP MAKING SENSE

alive which is a hugely liberating experience. Most of us will remember a pop concert, or a sporting event, where we felt completely transformed. For some reason or other, an atmosphere emerged in which we were able to completely lose ourselves.

In a world where our very existence as individuals inevitably leads us to live more and more separated from the real world and, therefore, feeling and sensation, we are desperate to find ways to reconnect. This is why humans have always expressed themselves artistically in one way or another, whether through music, painting, literature, or performance art. If you take a painting of water, for example by Monet, you are far more aware of all the minute undulations and shades of colour than if you had looked at that water yourself. The artist, who for some reason or other sees the extraordinary beauty and complexity of nature, is able to communicate that feeling through his painting. He is not representing "a piece of water" but the pond that he is looking at that very moment. He is capturing the unique and dynamic reality which he experienced. It is because we have lost the ability to perceive this living reality, that this type of painting can produce such strong emotions in us. Our conditioning expressed through the medium of language has blunted our perception of the world. We no longer look at everything as completely new and unique, but rather through the lens of abstraction. As a result, we are not seeing what is in front of our eyes, but instead an interpreted conditioned version. When we arrive somewhere new, the first thing we try to do is make sense of it, and give names to everything. We don't see its dynamic living character but instead try to fit it into the boxes which make up our reality. The more we understand and control our environment, the stronger this process gets, as we have removed as much spontaneity and uncertainty from our lives as possible. The result is that we are ever more cut off from life and seek to redress this balance as best we can.

One area where this is particularly obvious is extreme or dangerous activities. To my knowledge those living close to nature do not do this kind of thing. There is probably quite enough uncertainty and danger in simply surviving! If you hunt to survive (I am not talking about the modern hunter equipped with rifles), you are facing danger almost every time you go and do your weekly shop. Yet today in developed societies we are on the one hand completely obsessed with reducing danger as much as possible, a trend which is exemplified by the ever increasing and often absurd health and safety regulations, yet at the same time invent ever more extreme and dangerous sports. Where I live in the French Alps, I am constantly either coming across people who have been badly injured from sports or hearing about people dying. I am near a well-known "off-piste resort" called La Grave, where people are known to have slipped in narrow couloirs and skidded to their deaths on the rocks below. These deaths are not simply bad luck and unexpected, but a direct result of people pushing the limits. There was a ski teacher here who every summer would go off to the mountains

7. FREEDOM OR STOP MAKING SENSE

around the world in order to ski slopes steeper than 45 degrees. Inevitably he ended up being killed, and yet the ever-present danger of death must have been a large part of the reason he went. Paradoxically, the closer you are to death, the more alive you feel! This is a trend which has been accelerating recently, in, I believe, a direct response to the ever more controlled and safe environment which most people in more developed areas of the world live in. There has been an explosion in dangerous or at least adrenalin-pumping sports such as white-water rafting, sky-diving, canyoning, kite-surfing, rock-climbing and para-gliding to name but a few. Bungy jumping is another perfect example of this. I for one could never understand why anyone in their right mind would wish to jump into the void with only a harness and a piece of elastic band to save them from death. Yet the answer is perfectly obvious: they are simply trying to feel alive, to literally blast themselves into the present. There is no way that whilst you are falling to the ground at great speed, you are going to be worrying about paying your mortgage or any other of the millions of worries that plague us on a daily basis. Furthermore, you are intensely and completely aware of the present which is a huge relief. For a brief period (although time pretty much disappears in these kinds of situations) you are completely free. Yes, normal life comes crashing back into our consciousness after the euphoria has worn off, but this only encourages people to do it again. As our society has become more developed and our individuality has strengthened, our need for this kind of activity has increased.

Endurance sports are another way for people to liberate themselves from "reality", although the method is a different one. People who undertake extreme physical feats such as marathons and other types of endurance sports are generally admired, yet the reality is that one of the major reasons that people train and participate in these activities is in order to release endorphins or natural opiates. In fact, there are many people who become totally addicted to exercise because these endorphins are essentially very powerful opiate-type compounds produced by the body. They produce sensations of wellbeing and elation which enable sportspeople to temporarily leave the harsh world of problems behind. It is obviously not the same as an adrenalin rush from bio-chemical perspective, yet its effect, in as much as it helps you leave the humdrum of normal existence behind, is very similar. So, although from a societal perspective these activities are well considered, their purpose is very similar to drug use. All of them effectively release us from having to deal with the pain of our artificial separation. By making the present more intense and pleasant we simply leave all of the rest behind. This is the reason that people end up taking extreme amounts of exercise often to the detriment of their general health.

It is for exactly the same reasons that millions of people drink alcohol in all its forms, take cocaine, crack, heroin and all the other stimulants and mind-bending drugs which exist. It seems today that it is possible to be addicted to almost anything, including

7. FREEDOM OR STOP MAKING SENSE

pastimes which one might consider to be part of normal life such as eating and sex. Both of these pursuits will, by overwhelming our senses, provide temporary relief from our predicament. This probably is the reason that humans seem to indulge in ever more intense sexual practices. Sadomasochism is a case in point, where pain sometimes of an extreme nature is used to produce pleasure and relief. Just as in the case of Bungy jumping, being whipped will allow you to forget about having to go to work the next day! It is also clear from the obesity epidemic which is currently affecting people in developed economies across the globe, that overeating is a massive issue. The main culprit here seems to be refined sugars and corn syrup in particular, which has been put in a huge array of processed foods for the last 30 years or so. Refined sugar has a drug-like impact on the organism, producing temporary feelings of wellbeing and of course like all other drugs it wears off, thus requiring another dose. The result is an obesity epidemic, an explosion in type 2 (diet related) diabetes, and of course huge profits for the processed food industries. This type of food has become incredibly cheap, making it accessible to almost anybody. In complete contrast to the hyper sporty bunch, we have created a huge class of people who overeat mainly sugar-laden foods, take no exercise and spend their time watching TV or playing computer games. They will also often consume a lot of alcohol (containing more sugar) as well as other drugs such as cigarettes. All these different stimulants and drugs act together to blank life out either by temporarily making people feel better, or in the case of TV, enabling them to forget themselves. In fact, there seems to be a huge number of people who feel very unhappy if they are not being stimulated in some way or another. Many people will have the TV going in their houses practically 24/7 and would probably feel very uncomfortable spending time without at least some form of outside stimulation.

Yet it is clear that we are not all addicts and many of us are able to live without the need for endlessly more extreme sensations. So how do those who aren't attracted by drugs or extreme sensations cope? In what way do they manage to dissolve their individuality even temporarily? For me the most obvious root is clearly creative expression in all its forms. Although today we view art mostly as spectators, before the modern era all the creative mediums existed in the context of their communities. This is still very much the case in parts of the world such as rural Africa where music and dancing are part of life. The villagers are not spectators but both the creators and participants. It is a mechanism by which they can lose themselves in the moment whilst expressing their emotions directly. Dancing is a very good example of this and has been part of human culture since time immemorial. It is an activity which forces you to be aware of your body and the music you are listening to and also allows you to be completely taken over by it. In effect you can become one with the music and the movement, with feeling and sensation taking over from thinking. Of course, dancing can range from being very formal and technique-based as

7. FREEDOM OR STOP MAKING SENSE

exemplified by ballet to completely free-form. Yet I am sure that even highly formalised and technique-based dance can be liberating, once the dancer fully lets go. In fact, this type of situation is repeated across a whole range of activities which require a lot of training such as tennis, football, squash or any other competitive sport. Once the technique becomes fully integrated then the performer/sportsperson can begin to really become part of the movement. This is not only associated with a very high skill level but also with a very pleasurable sense of completely letting go. If you take a game like tennis, for example, it is only when you are good enough to actually trust your movements that you can start to let go enough to play well. It is the sensation of easy and flowing movement, which enables you to play effectively and exist in the here and now. Skiing is a sport where this situation is obvious, because it is all about trusting your skis and their movement. Once you have learnt to feel and trust the way your skis react and your legs are fit enough to cope with absorbing the shocks, you can just go with it. This gives you a real sense of freedom and wellbeing, not only because you feel alive but also because you are not having to mentally control everything. Yes, you are still reacting and adjusting but as part of a process which you are having to cede to. As with tennis, the more you stop trying to minutely control it and just ride the sensations, the better and more in control you are. On a ski slope it is clear that those who are trying to completely control their skis are the beginners who are most out of control. The situation as with most things in life is completely paradoxical, as it is by giving up mental control that you gain physical control. This must be the reason that sport in all its forms has become ever more popular. It is a rediscovery of our physicality and of our presence in the here and now. You are not going to do very well in your tennis match if you are thinking of the future or the past! The better you become and the more relaxed you are when you play, the more intense the moment becomes and the more the artificial world disappears.

This also applies to all the different forms of artistic expression such as music, the visual arts, poetry, and literature. Music, for example, as with physical movement directly stimulates our senses both as a performer or listener, bringing us back to the moment. It enables us to live through our senses rather than our intellect, thus temporarily enabling us to rediscover reality. Of course, music has an intellectual side and is often telling a story or sending us a message, but in general it speaks to us from a different place. Why else would humans have started to make music? It seems to exist in virtually all civilizations and must therefore be an integral part of what it means to be human. Because we have cut ourselves off through our imaginary shared world, we have felt the need to produce sounds which are more intense than those made by nature. Today almost wherever you go, in your car, your house, the supermarket, or walking around, we are surrounded by music. For many to simply "be" in silence is unbearable which is why you see so many people walking around with iPods and other mobile music devices. Most of

7. FREEDOM OR STOP MAKING SENSE

these people simply need sensorial stimulation, yet others find that music soothes and relaxes them. It is well known that the music of Mozart helps babies fall asleep, whilst for many adults his music takes them out of themselves to another place. Ironically enough, Mozart himself clearly found life very difficult which might on the surface seem surprising. Yet there are many examples in history of great artists whose work transforms people's perception yet found life to be full of hardship and suffering. Van Gogh is a classic example of this; a man who was incredibly aware of the beauty, complexity and dynamic nature of life yet found life to be full of pain. Perhaps it is because he was so aware of the discrepancy between the real reality and normal life that he both suffered and produced such extraordinary works of art. These artists don't need to understand this paradox from an intellectual perspective but are just finding a way of coping. Artists can often be very troubled people, forced to find an artistic outlet in order to cope. Yet for many, including Van Gogh, even art does not enable them to square the circle and they end up taking their own lives in one way or another.

The written word is another means by which it is possible to transcend "normality". This might on the surface seem odd in that unlike with music, dance or painting you are relying completely on mental images. Yet we all know that words, just as much as a painting, are able to transport us out of our current situation. Most literature is no different to TV or canned music, in that by distracting us it enables us to escape our humdrum world, yet great literature just like great music or painting can be spiritually uplifting. Perhaps the classic example of this is in Marcel Proust's "Swan's Way", where he completely brings to life the sensations and feeling associated with tasting his aunt's "madeleine" (a shell like sponge cake) as a young child. What talks to us, is not his personal experience, but the overwhelming nature of the sensations and the "now" which are being recalled. Smell and taste are incredible powerful sensations which are very strongly associated with memory and it is this which he is triggering in the reader. He recreates a feeling of an intensely dense and real present; something children experience much more than adults. In this way he uses writing to reawaken feelings inside us which have been buried by the crushing weight of ordinary life. Thus, great writing can touch us just as much as great art or music, as it reawakens in us the joy of being truly alive. For me there is almost no better example of this than the opening pages of John Steinbeck's Cannery Row. (15)

"Cannery Row in Monterey in California is a poem, a stink, a grating noise, a quality of light, a tone, a habit, a nostalgia, a dream. Cannery Row is the gathered and scattered tin and iron and rust and splintered wood, chipped pavement and weedy lots and junk heaps, sardine canneries of corrugated iron, honky tonks, restaurants and whore houses and little crowded groceries and laboratories and flop houses. Its inhabitants are as the man once said, "whores, pimps, gamblers and sons of bitches" by which he meant Everybody. Had the man

7. FREEDOM OR STOP MAKING SENSE

looked through another peep-hole he might have said: "Saints and angels and martyrs and holy men" and he would have meant the same thing."

To me this passage awakens an awareness of the transient, incomprehensible yet very real nature of our existence. A place is brought to life that exists but from a million different angles and points of view that are in perpetual motion. The same effect can be found in poetry, which smashes the humdrum of ordinary life.

> *Hold fast to dreams*
> *For if dreams die*
> *Life is a broken-winged bird*
> *That cannot fly.*
> *Hold fast to dreams*
> *For when dreams go*
> *Life is a barren field*
> *Frozen with snow.*
>
> *Langston Hughes*

So it seems that whilst on an intellectual level at least we are able to believe in our illusory world and regard it as THE reality despite all the obvious discrepancies which might lead one to question it, on an emotional and intuitive level this is simply not possible. There have, of course, always been people who can see through the illusion, but they are definitely a minority and are often persecuted. Yet for many, physical and artistic expression enables a reconnection with a life free from any kind of questioning. They are simply taken over by the creative process, and temporarily liberated from their cage. Many other people as I have described, cope by anaesthetizing themselves in one way or another, and escaping from the suffering of their daily lives. So, in one way or another we are all finding the best way of coping with an impossible situation. We are essentially one great invention yet at the same time it is that very invention that has enabled us to be so successful. Furthermore, the invention was not dreamt up last week but is at the very origin of human existence on Earth. We haven't chosen our situation but are simply doing the best we can, whether it is by inventing notions such as religion and morality, or trying to reconnect with reality through art or movement.

It is clear that there is no easy solution to the paradox that is the human condition and that our lives will continue to be a mix of suffering and freedom. Our conditioning and situation force us to live within the confines of our artificial world, whilst our thirst for true freedom leads us to find ways of reconnecting with the whole. It also appears that direct attempts to break free from the human condition via spiritual practices are likely to end in failure. Yes, there will always be a few examples of people who seem to be able to live more or less entirely in the here and now, but they are extremely rare. Furthermore, even these people are likely to find their conditioning will continue to create some difficulties for them.

7. FREEDOM OR STOP MAKING SENSE

Given this situation, is there no hope and are we simply condemned to accept our lot? In a sense yes, because there is clearly no grand "solution" or "path" by which we will be able to resolve the paradox. The moment we try to find one, we immediately find ourselves in the trap of our illusory existence as individuals. What, however, there is for each and every one of us, at every moment of our conscious existence, is the possibility of changing our perspective, or to stop *trying* to make sense, and this is why I wrote this book. To be aware of *"real reality"* in the words of Octavio Paz does not require discipline or years of practice, but simply a different perspective. *"Reality"* is in fact right there, under our noses all the time, and we simply have to let it touch us. All our striving, wanting, training is simply a distraction and will lead us nowhere other than to more frustration and desire. So, although I cannot give you any kind of road map, I can at least reassure you that you are always free to reconnect and be whole. With this in mind, the next time you are swept away by a view, a piece of music, a sense of peace or simple contentedness, perhaps you will realise that you are privileged enough to be experiencing the extraordinary beauty of life.

REFERENCES

1. Letter to the family of his friend Michele Besso from Albert Einstein, after Besso's death in 1955.

2. Carlo Rovelli; Forget Time, published 24th August 2008- *http://fqxi.org/data/essay-contest-files/ Rovelli_Time.pdf*

3. Richard Feynman, The Feynman Lectures on Physics: Quantum mechanics
   Richard Phillips Feynman, Robert B. Leighton, Matthew Linzee Sands
   Addison-Wesley Pub. Co., 1965

4. Unsourced quote from Albert Einstein

5. Synchronicity: An Acausal Connecting Principle by C G Jung, Publisher: Bollingen; [1st Princeton/ Bollingen paperback edition (December 1, 1973) ISBN-10: 0691017948 ISBN-13: 978-0691017945

REFERENCES

6. From, William Shakespeare's Hamlet Act 3

7. Declaration of the Rights of Man and of the Citizen 1789
   http://en.wikipedia.org/wiki/Declaration_of_the_Rights_of_Man_and_of_the_Citizen

8. Professor of Physiology at the Los Angeles School of medicine, in a paper published in 1987 called "The worst mistake in the history of the human race"

9. Why the Hadza are Still Hunter-Gatherer, Frank Marlowe, Department of Anthropology, Harvard University 2002. in Ethnicity, Hunter-Gatherers, and the "Other": Association or Assimilation in Africa, Sue Kent (Ed.) Washington D.C.: Smithsonian Institution Press, pp. 247-275.

10. *http://newsfeed.time.com/2011/05/26/amazonian-tribe-lacks-abstract-concept-of-time/*

11. **The Gay Science** (*German:* **Die fröhliche Wissenschaft**) is a book written by *Friedrich Nietzsche,* first published in 1882 and followed by a second edition, which was published after the completion of *Thus Spoke Zarathustra* and *Beyond Good and Evil,* in 1887. *http://en.wikipedia.org/wiki/The_Gay_Science*

12. *www.bloomberg.com/.../france-u-s-have-highest-depression-rates-in-...*
    26 Jul 2011 – More people reported being depressed in France and the U.S. than anywhere in ... to the study, published July 25 in the journal BMC Medicine

13. **Octavio Paz's – "In search of the present" 1990 Nobel Literature Prize Lecture** *http://www.nobelprize.org/nobel_prizes/literature/laureates/1990/paz-lecture.html*

14. J.Krishnamurti- The Core of the Teachings © 1993 The Krishnamurti Foundation Trust Ltd, Brockwood Park, Bramdean, Hampshire, England.

15. John Steinbeck, Cannery Row, first printed 1945, ISBN: 0553266039 / 0-553-26603-9

www.ingramcontent.com/pod-product-compliance
Lightning Source LLC
Chambersburg PA
CBHW022112040426
42450CB00006B/672